Teaching Differently Intentionally: A Framework for Transforming Education

written by Alisa L. Grace

© 2024 Alisa L. Grace
All rights reserved.

No part of this book may be reproduced in any form or by any electronic or mechanical means, including information storage and retrieval systems, without permission in writing from the publisher.

Self-Published by
Alisa L. Grace
Sanford, FL 32771

ISBN: 978-1-966129-11-0

First Edition

Printed in the United States of America

Library of Congress Cataloging-in-Publication Data
Grace, Alisa L.
Title of the Book: Teaching Differently Intentionally A Framework for Transforming Education
Library of Congress Control Number: 2024923769

Disclaimer: The views expressed in this book are those of the author and do not necessarily reflect any organizations or individuals mentioned.

Acknowledgments: The author wishes to thank God, Her Husband (Linion), Victory Temple of God, Florida SPECS, Unity Youth Association, All About Serving You, Angels-ANJ Events, NordeVest, and Love & Create Life for their support and contributions.

This Book is dedicated to

To my dearly beloved Heavenly Father, I am honored you chose me for this task. You have been with me throughout the entire process of guiding and leading me, and I am forever grateful for your everlasting support.

To our dedicated educators who have chosen this mission of educating our youth and want to enhance their teaching skills.

To the students who have given it their all yet feel defeated. We understand your struggle and offer a solution.

Table of Contents

Dear Teachers and Parents 9

Decision-Making Survey: Is *Teach Differently Intentionally* Right for You? 13

Student Decision-Making Survey: Is *Teaching Differently Intentionally* Right for You? 19

Introduction 27

Chapter 1: The Need for a New Approach 29

PART ONE: UNDERSTANDING THE STRUGGLE 35

Chapter 2: Why Students Struggle with Learning 37

    Identifying the Issues 41

    Case Studies: Real Students, Real Struggles 42

    Addressing the Root Causes 43

Chapter 3: The Impact of Traditional Teaching on Students 45

    The Emotional Toll 48

    Academic Outcomes 48

    A Call for Change: Teaching Differently Intentionally 49

Chapter 4: A New Perspective: The Power of Intention in Teaching 51

    Defining Intentional Teaching 54

    Benefits of Intentional Teaching 55

    Embracing a New Perspective 56

PART TWO: THE TEACHING DIFFERENTLY INTENTIONALLY FRAMEWORK 57

Chapter 5: Understanding the Framework 59

    Overview of the Methodology 62

    Framework Components 62

    A Framework for Transformation 65

Chapter 6: How Do You Learn? Survey 67

    Importance of Understanding Learning Styles 70

    Implementation: Administering the How Do You Learn? Survey 71

    The Transformative Power of Understanding Learning Styles 73

Chapter 7: Creating a Conducive Learning Environment 75

    Classroom Dynamics 78

Essential Tools 79
Building a Conducive Learning Environment 81

Chapter 8: Start with the Test Content 83
Reverse Engineering Learning 86
Practical Application 87
The Benefits of Reverse Engineering Learning 88
Integrating Reverse Engineering Learning into Your Teaching 89

PART THREE: STRATEGIES FOR ENGAGEMENT AND SUCCESS 91

Chapter 9: Interactive Activities for Memorable Learning 93
Engagement Techniques 96
Real-World Connections 98
The Transformative Power of Interactive and Real-World Learning 100

Chapter 10: Continuous Progress Monitoring 103
Importance of Ongoing Assessment 106
Tools and Techniques for Effective Progress Monitoring 107

Chapter 11: Presenting Learning in Their Way 111

Unleashing Student Potential: Diverse Paths to Learning 117
Rubric-Based Assessment: Encouraging Creativity and Ownership 118

PART FOUR: IMPLEMENTING AND REFLECTING 121

Chapter 12: Testing the Learning Process 123
Assessment Tools and Technologies 127
Selecting the Right Assessment Tools 128
Using Assessment Data to Inform Instruction 129

Chapter 13: Concluding with Learning 131
Celebrating Success: Fostering a Positive Learning Environment 135

CONCLUSION 137

Chapter 14: The Future of Education 139

APPENDICES 145
Appendix A: Sample Survey for Learning Styles 149
Appendix B: Sample Rubrics 153
Appendix C: Resources for Interactive Activities 161

Appendix D: Reflection and Progress Monitoring Tools **165**
    Understanding Reflection and Progress Monitoring 166
    Student Reflection Tools... 166
    Teacher Progress Monitoring Tools 167
    Collaborative Reflection Tools 168
    Goal Setting Worksheet... 169

Student-Created Reflection Questions Form..**171**
    Reflect on your learning: 171

Peer Feedback Form **173**
    Student Name: Project/Assignment: 173

Meet the Author: Alisa Ladawn Grace **175**

Dear Teachers and Parents

I hope this letter finds you well and inspired as we embark on a journey to transform the educational experience for our children. I want to begin by emphasizing that *Teaching Differently Intentionally* is not a curriculum but a methodology—a flexible framework that can be used with any curriculum you currently use. This guide offers a fresh, new way of teaching and learning, designed to benefit teachers and students by enhancing the educational process in meaningful and impactful ways.

Why This Is Important

In today's rapidly changing world, traditional teaching methods have failed to address the diverse needs of our students. Many children struggle to connect with the material, leading to disengagement, frustration, and a lack of academic growth. Parents and educators have witnessed firsthand how this can affect a child's confidence and love for learning.

Teaching Differently Intentionally is not just another teaching method; it is a deliberate, thoughtful approach that prioritizes each student's unique learning styles, interests, and abilities. By shifting from a one-size-fits-all model to a more personalized, interactive, and exploratory approach, we can create an environment that fosters values, understanding, and empowerment for each child to reach their full potential.

The Importance of These Methods

At School:

Teaching Differently Intentionally fosters an engaging and dynamic learning environment in the classroom. The seamless integration of exploration, interactive activities, and real-world applications ensures that students actively engage in learning. This approach ensures that students take an active role in their educational journey, moving beyond passive reception of information to become empowered participants in their learning process. This approach improves academic outcomes and instills a sense of ownership and pride in their achievements.

At Home:

As parents, you play a critical role in reinforcing what your child learns at school. The principles of *Teaching Differently Intentionally* can be seamlessly integrated into everyday life, making learning a continuous and enjoyable process. By encouraging exploration and supporting your child's interests, they will develop a love for learning that extends beyond the classroom.

In the Community:

Learning continues beyond the school gates. Our communities have opportunities for children to apply what they've learned meaningfully. Revitalizing instruction and learning through this approach can help students positively impact the world around them, whether through community projects, volunteering, or local events.

The Utility of These Methods

The beauty of *Teaching Differently Intentionally* lies in its versatility. This methodology is designed to be adaptable, allowing educators and parents to tailor it to the specific needs of their students and children, giving them a sense of empowerment and control over the educational process.

Moreover, this method prepares students not just for tests but for life. By focusing on critical thinking, problem-solving, and collaboration, we endeavor to equip our children with the skills to navigate a world that is progressively intricate and interlinked adeptly. These skills will empower them to succeed not only in their academic pursuits but also in their personal and professional lives.

In Conclusion

As educators and parents, we can create a transformative learning experience that will benefit our children for years. Let's work hand in hand to foster an environment where every child can discover the joy of learning and realize their full potential, sparking a sense of excitement and motivation for their educational journey.

Thank you for your dedication and commitment to our children's future. I look forward to working together as we embark on this exciting journey of educational transformation.

Warm regards,

Alisa L. Grace
Author/Curriculum Specialist/Transformational Life Coach
Sir-Rendered For Life, LLC

Decision-Making Survey: Is *Teach Differently Intentionally* Right for You?

This survey is designed to help **teachers and parents** assess whether the *Teaching Differently Intentionally* methodology aligns with their goals and needs for enhancing the learning experience of their students and children.

Section 1: Current Teaching and Learning Experience

1. **How would you describe your current approach to teaching or supporting your child's education?**

    ☐ Traditional and structured
    ☐ Mixed, with some hands-on activities
    ☐ Primarily interactive and student-centered
    ☐ Other: _____

2. **How satisfied are you with your students/child's academic progress using the current teaching methods?**

    ☐ Very satisfied
    ☐ Satisfied
    ☐ Neutral
    ☐ Dissatisfied
    ☐ Very dissatisfied

3. **Do your students/children often feel stressed or anxious about tests and assessments?**

    ☐ Always
    ☐ Often

☐ Sometimes

☐ Rarely

☐ Never

4. **How engaged are your students/children in their learning?**

   ☐ Very engaged

   ☐ Somewhat engaged

   ☐ Neutral

   ☐ Disengaged

   ☐ Very disengaged

Section 2: Educational Goals and Challenges

5. **What are your primary goals for your students/child in their educational journey? (Select all that apply)**

   ☐ Academic excellence

   ☐ Emotional well-being and confidence

   ☐ Critical thinking and problem-solving skills

   ☐ Creativity and innovation

   ☐ Real-world application of knowledge

   ☐ Other: _____

6. **What challenges are you currently facing in teaching or supporting your child's education? (Select all that apply)**

   ☐ Lack of engagement

   ☐ Difficulty connecting learning to real-life situations

   ☐ Test anxiety and performance issues

   ☐ Inadequate academic progress

   ☐ Difficulty catering to different learning styles

   ☐ Other: _____

7. How open are you to new teaching or learning methods that differ from traditional approaches?

    ☐ Very open
    ☐ Somewhat open
    ☐ Neutral
    ☐ Reluctant
    ☐ Very reluctant

Section 3: Alignment with Teach Differently Intentionally

8. Do students learn best through exploration, interactive activities, and real-world applications?

    ☐ Strongly agree
    ☐ Agree
    ☐ Neutral
    ☐ Disagree
    ☐ Strongly disagree

9. How important is it to you that teaching methods adapt to the unique learning styles and needs of each student/child?

    ☐ Very important
    ☐ Important
    ☐ Neutral
    ☐ Not very important
    ☐ Not important at all

10. Would you like a methodology that prepares students for tests and real-life challenges?

    ☐ Very interested
    ☐ Interested
    ☐ Neutral

☐ Not very interested

☐ Not interested at all

11. **How likely are you to implement or support a teaching approach that emphasizes the student's role as an active participant in their learning?**

    ☐ Very Likely

    ☐ Likely

    ☐ Neutral

    ☐ Unlikely

    ☐ Very unlikely

Section 4: Reflection and Decision

12. **Based on your responses, do your current methods fully support your students'/child's potential?**

    ☐ Yes

    ☐ No

    ☐ Unsure

13. **After completing this survey, could *Teaching Differently Intentionally* address your challenges and help you achieve your educational goals?**

    ☐ Yes

    ☐ No

    ☐ Unsure

14. **How willing are you to explore and potentially adopt the *Teach Differently Intentionally* methodology?**

    ☐ Very willing

    ☐ Somewhat willing

    ☐ Neutral

    ☐ Reluctant

    ☐ Not willing at all

Section 5: Next Steps

15. Would you like to receive more information or participate in a workshop to learn how to implement *Teaching Differently Intentionally*?

☐ Yes, please provide more information

☐ Yes, I'd like to attend a workshop

☐ No, I'm not interested at this time

Additional Comments:

_____

_____

_____

Survey Conclusion: Thank you for taking the time to complete this survey. Your responses will help determine if the *Teaching Differently Intentionally* methodology fits you and your students/children. Whether you decide to move forward with this approach or not, your commitment to improving education is commendable, and we are here to support you in any way we can.

Warm regards,

Alisa L. Grace
Author/Curriculum Specialist/Transformational Life Coach
Sir-Rendered For Life, LLC
sirrenderedforlife.com

Student Decision-Making Survey: Is *Teaching Differently Intentionally* Right for You?

This survey is designed to help you, as a **student**, think about how you learn best and whether the *Teaching Differently Intentionally* method could help you succeed in your studies.

Section 1: Your Current Learning Experience

1. **How do you feel about your classes right now?**

   ☐ I enjoy them and feel engaged.
   ☐ They're okay but sometimes dull.
   ☐ I often feel bored or uninterested.
   ☐ I find them challenging and stressful.

2. **How well do you understand the material you're learning in school?**

   ☐ I understand everything clearly.
   ☐ I understand most things, but some are confusing.
   ☐ I struggle to understand some of the material.
   ☐ I often don't understand what I'm being taught.

3. **Do you feel stressed or anxious about tests and exams?**

   ☐ Always
   ☐ Often
   ☐ Sometimes
   ☐ Rarely
   ☐ Never

4. How much do you enjoy hands-on activities, like experiments, projects, or creative assignments?

☐ I love them—they're my favorite!
☐ I like them sometimes.
☐ I prefer traditional learning (like reading and listening to lectures).
☐ I don't enjoy hands-on activities.

Section 2: Your Learning Preferences

5. What type of learning activities do you enjoy the most? (Select all that apply)

☐ Working on group projects
☐ Doing experiments or practical tasks
☐ Reading and writing
☐ Watching videos or listening to explanations
☐ Creating things (art, models, presentations)
☐ Other: _____

6. How do you like to study for tests?

☐ I like to review notes and textbooks.
☐ I prefer using flashcards or study apps.
☐ I study best by doing practice tests or quizzes.
☐ I like discussing the material with friends or teachers.
☐ Other: _____

7. Do you find learning easier when relating the material to real-life situations?

☐ Yes, it helps me understand better.
☐ Sometimes, but not always.
☐ Not really, I prefer straightforward teaching.
☐ No, I don't see the connection.

Section 3: Your Thoughts on Teaching Differently

8. **Would you like to try a learning method focusing on hands-on activities, exploration, and real-world applications?**

    ☐ Definitely!

    ☐ I think so; it sounds interesting.

    ☐ I'm not sure, but I'm open to it.

    ☐ Not really; I prefer traditional methods.

9. **How do you feel about being more involved in choosing how you learn and how you show what you've learned?**

    ☐ I would love to have more choice and control.

    ☐ I think it would be helpful sometimes.

    ☐ I prefer it when the teacher decides everything.

    ☐ I'm not interested in making those decisions.

10. **Can you start with what will be on a test and then learn the material in a fun and interactive way?**

    ☐ Yes, that sounds great!

    ☐ Maybe I'd have to try it.

    ☐ I don't think that would make a difference.

    ☐ No, I prefer learning differently.

Section 4: Reflection and Decision

11. **Do you feel like the way you're currently learning is helping you reach your full potential?**

    ☐ Yes, I feel like I'm doing my best.

    ☐ Sometimes, but I think I could do better.

    ☐ No, I think I could be learning more.

    ☐ I'm not sure.

12. After completing this survey, could the *Teaching Differently Intentionally* method help you learn better and enjoy school more?

☐ Yes, it seems like a good fit for me.

☐ Maybe I'd like to learn more about it.

☐ I'm not sure, but I'm curious.

☐ No, I think I prefer my current way of learning.

13. How willing are you to try the *Teaching Differently Intentionally* method to see if it works for you?

☐ Very willing

☐ Somewhat willing

☐ Not sure

☐ Not willing

Section 5: Next Steps

14. Would you like to discuss this method with your teacher or parent to learn how it might help you?

☐ Yes, I'd like to talk about it.

☐ Maybe I'm interested in learning more.

☐ No, I'm not interested.

Additional Comments:

_____

_____

_____

_____

_____

Survey Conclusion: Thank you for taking the time to complete this survey. Your responses will help you and your teachers/parents determine if the *Teaching Differently Intentionally* method might fit your learning style and needs well. Remember, the goal is to find the best way to help you succeed and enjoy your learning experience.

Best regards,

Alisa L. Grace
Author/Curriculum Specialist/Transformational Life Coach
Sir-Rendered For Life, LLC
sirrenderedforlife.com

Introducing Teaching Differently Intentionally, a concept developed by Alisa L. Grace, an educator with extensive experience and a passion for transformative teaching.

While not every child may possess exceptional innate talents, every child deserves the chance to explore their potential and thrive in a student-centered educational environment.

Introduction

Welcome to the *Teaching Differently Intentionally* Guide

Dear Teachers and Parents,

Welcome to the *Teaching Differently Intentionally* guide, a resource designed to help you create a more engaging, effective, and personalized learning experience for your students and children. Whether you're an educator looking to refresh your teaching methods or a Homeschool parent seeking to support your child's education better, this guide provides a versatile framework that can easily be tailored to complement any existing curriculum. Our goal is simple: to provide tools and strategies that make learning more meaningful, enjoyable, and successful for every student. By embracing this intentional approach, we can help each child discover their unique potential and thrive academically and personally.

Thank you for joining us on this journey to transform education and make a lasting impact on our children's future.

Introduction:
Chapter 1: The Need for a New Approach

A teacher's frustration mirrors the stagnant progress of diverse students. It's time for a change!

Despite the dedication and countless training sessions, many educators see stagnant or minimal growth in their students' academic achievements.

Chapter 1: The Need for a New Approach

The Problem with Traditional Teaching: Despite the dedication and countless training sessions, many educators see stagnant or minimal growth in their students' academic achievements.

The Vision Behind Teaching Differently Intentionally: Introduce the concept developed by Alisa L. Grace, an educator with extensive experience and a passion for transformative teaching.

Chapter 1:
The Need for a New Approach

The Stagnation in Traditional Teaching

In classrooms across the country, a persistent problem lingers—an issue that has frustrated educators and disheartened students for generations. Despite the dedication, passion, and countless hours of professional development, many teachers stare at data that reflects stagnant or minimal growth in their students' academic achievements. It's a disheartening reality, especially for those who entered the profession with a deep desire to inspire and uplift young minds.

This is not for lack of effort. Teachers pour their hearts into lesson plans, spend evenings grading papers, and participate in training designed to enhance their skills. Yet, something crucial is missing. Too often, traditional teaching methods—those rooted in lectures, rote memorization, and standardized testing—fail to engage students or ignite their natural curiosity. These methods have left many students feeling disillusioned, disconnected, and disempowered.

Voices of Frustration: The Students' Perspective

Alisa L. Grace, an experienced educator passionate about transformative teaching, has heard the cries of frustration from students all too often: *"I do well in class, but I can't pass the test." "I am bored because of the constant lecturing." "I know the content, but I don't like how I have to provide the answer."* These complaints are not just gripes; they echo a deeper issue within the educational system—a system often prioritizes conformity over creativity, standardization over individualized learning, and testing over proper understanding.

The Limitations of Traditional Methods

Alisa recognized that these issues stemmed from the traditional teaching approach, which has remained unchanged for decades. She saw that this approach failed to meet modern students' needs and contributed to a growing frustration among educators who felt powerless to effect real change. The time had come for a new way forward—a way that would honor the diverse needs of students, reignite their passion for learning and empower teachers to make a difference truly.

The Birth of Teaching Differently Intentionally

And so, the vision for *Teaching Differently Intentionally* was born. This innovative approach, developed by Alisa L. Grace, addresses the core problems inherent in traditional teaching practices that need to focus on underlying issues such as the joy of learning, the power of exploration, and the importance of intentional, student-centered instruction.

A Vision for Transformative Teaching

Alisa's vision is clear: to alleviate the frustration that plagues teaching and learning by providing a methodology that embraces exploration, interactive activities, and real-world applications. *Teaching Differently Intentionally* is not just another set of teaching strategies; it is a transformative way of thinking about education. It challenges the status quo and invites educators to see their role not merely as dispensers of knowledge but as guides, facilitators, and partners in the learning journey.

The Call for a New Educational Paradigm

This first chapter will explore the underlying issues that necessitate a new approach to education. We will examine why traditional methods have fallen short and why we must embrace a new, more intentional way of teaching. The journey ahead is one of transformation—transformation in how we teach, how students learn, and ultimately, how we prepare the next generation for a world that demands creativity, critical thinking, and a deep love for learning.

Moving Forward with Teaching Differently Intentionally

An innovative approach is necessary, and *Teaching Differently Intentionally* provides the solution. It is time to surpass the constraints of the past and confidently embrace a future where each student can thrive in a learning environment intentionally designed to facilitate their growth and enable them to reach their utmost potential. This marks the commencement of that transformative journey.

Part One:

Understanding the Struggle

Chapter 2: Why Students Struggle with Learning

Overwhelmed and disconnected, students grapple with varied learning styles and anxieties.

Students who struggled in traditional classrooms have thrived with alternative teaching approaches, such as project-based learning and mastery-based grading.

Chapter 2:
Why Students Struggle with Learning

Identifying the Issues: Explore common reasons students struggle, including diverse learning styles, disengagement, and test anxiety.

Case Studies: Provide examples of students who have struggled under traditional methods and how their issues were addressed through different teaching approaches.

Chapter 2:
Why Students Struggle with Learning

Identifying the Issues

Every classroom presents teachers with diverse students, each with unique strengths, challenges, and learning styles. Despite this diversity, traditional educational models continue with the one-size-fits-all teaching method, which can lead to significant struggles for many students. Understanding why students struggle is the first step toward creating more effective and inclusive learning environments.

Diverse Learning Styles

One of the most significant challenges in education is accommodating students' diverse learning styles. Some students thrive in a visual learning environment, while others excel through auditory or kinesthetic experiences. Traditional teaching methods, which rely heavily on lectures and textbooks, may only cater to a fraction of the classroom. As a result, students whose learning styles differ from the dominant method may struggle to grasp the material, not because they lack ability but because the information is not presented in a way that aligns with how they learn best.

Disengagement and Boredom

Another common issue is student disengagement. When lessons are not interactive or relevant to students' lives, they can quickly lose interest. This disengagement often manifests as boredom, lack of participation, or behavioral problems. Students may feel that what they are learning has no real-world application, leading them to question the value of their education. When students are disengaged, they are less likely to retain information, perform well on assessments, or develop a love for learning.

Test Anxiety and Performance Pressure

Test anxiety is another critical factor that contributes to student struggles. The pressure to perform well on standardized tests and exams can overwhelm many students. This anxiety can cloud their thinking, disrupt their concentration, and ultimately lead to poor performance, even if they understand the material. The high stakes associated with these tests can cause students to focus more on the fear of failure than on the process of learning, creating a cycle of anxiety and underachievement.

Case Studies: Real Students, Real Struggles

Case Study 1: Na'ima's Journey from Disengagement to Engagement

Na'ima was a bright student with a natural curiosity about the world. However, her grades didn't reflect her potential. Traditional classroom settings left her bored and unmotivated. She often felt disconnected from the material and struggled to see its relevance to her life. Her disengagement led to declining grades and a growing sense of frustration.

This changed when Na'ima's teacher implemented a more interactive and personalized approach. Instead of relying solely on lectures, the teacher incorporated project-based learning, where Na'ima could explore topics she was passionate about. By connecting the curriculum to real-world scenarios and allowing Na'ima to take ownership of her knowledge, the teacher was able to reignite her interest. Na'ima's grades improved, but more importantly, she rediscovered her love for learning.

Case Study 2: Noah's Battle with Test Anxiety

Noah was a diligent student who excelled in classwork but consistently underperformed on tests. Despite understanding the material, he would freeze up during exams, unable to recall information or think clearly. The pressure to perform well only increased his anxiety, blocking the knowledge he learned and leaving him to focus on dreading every test.

Recognizing the root of Noah's struggles, his teacher introduced alternative assessment methods. Instead of relying solely on traditional tests, the teacher incorporated oral presentations, creative projects, and open-book assessments. These alternative methods allowed Noah to demonstrate his knowledge without the overwhelming pressure of a timed test. Over time, as Noah built confidence in these low-stakes environments, his test anxiety lessened, and he also began to perform better on traditional assessments.

Case Study 3: Nyrie's Struggle with Learning Styles

Nyrie needed help to keep up with his peers in a lecture-heavy environment. While his classmates seemed to grasp concepts quickly through verbal explanations, Nyrie found it challenging to process information this way. He often felt left behind and started believing he wasn't as bright as the others.

Nyrie's teacher recognized that he might have a different learning style and began incorporating more visual aids, hands-on activities, and group work into the lessons. By presenting information in various ways, the teacher created an inclusive classroom environment where Nyrie could thrive. As a result, Nyrie's understanding of the material deepened, and his confidence grew.

Addressing the Root Causes

These case studies illustrate that students' struggles often stem from a mismatch between their needs and the teaching methods. Whether it's accommodating diverse learning styles, addressing disengagement, or reducing test anxiety, the key to helping students succeed lies in understanding and addressing these root causes.

Teaching Differently Intentionally recognizes that every student is unique and that their struggles are often symptoms of a more significant issue within the traditional educational system. By adopting a more flexible, personalized approach to teaching, educators can create environments where all students can thrive, regardless of their challenges.

In the following chapters, we will explore how to implement these strategies in the classroom and provide practical tools to help educators transform their teaching and, ultimately, their students' learning experiences. The goal is not just to help students pass tests but to help them become confident, engaged learners who are prepared for success beyond the classroom.

Notes:

Chapter 3: The Impact of Traditional Teaching on Students

Bored and defeated, students feel the weight of conventional teaching methods.

The Emotional Toll: Traditional methods can create stress, impacting students' well-being and love for learning.
Academic Outcomes: Traditional approaches can limit critical thinking and deep understanding, hindering long-term academic success.

Chapter 3:
The Impact of Traditional Teaching on Students

The Emotional Toll: Discuss how traditional methods can leave students feeling defeated and disconnected.

Academic Outcomes: Review the impact of conventional approaches on test scores and overall learning retention.

Chapter 3:
The Impact of Traditional Teaching on Students

The Emotional Toll

In the quest to educate and prepare students for the future, traditional teaching methods have often overlooked a crucial aspect of the learning experience: students' emotional well-being. Reliance on lectures, rote memorization, and standardized testing can leave many students feeling defeated, disconnected, and disillusioned about their education.

The pressure to conform to rigid expectations can be overwhelming for some students. When their unique learning needs are unmet, they may internalize feelings of inadequacy, believing they are not intelligent or capable enough to succeed. This sense of failure can erode their self-esteem, leading to a lack of motivation and a growing disengagement from school.

Traditional teaching methods often prioritize content delivery over meaningful interaction, creating a disconnect between students and their teachers. Without opportunities for students to actively participate, ask questions, or explore topics in a way that resonates with them, the classroom can become an isolating place. Students frequently experience a sense of being passive receivers of information instead of being engaged contributors in their educational experience when more connectivity is required. The emotional toll of traditional teaching is not just felt in the classroom; it extends beyond the school walls. Students who feel defeated by their educational experiences may carry these feelings into other areas of their lives, affecting their relationships, extracurricular activities, and overall sense of self-worth. Over time, the cumulative effect of these emotional struggles can lead to a deep-seated aversion to learning and resistance to educational opportunities in the future.

Academic Outcomes

While the emotional impact of traditional teaching methods is profound, the academic outcomes are equally concerning. Many students believe that standardized testing is an important measure of success, but they also feel the pressure to improve their performance on these assessments and gain a deeper understanding of the material. The pressure to memorize and regurgitate information for exams can hinder proper comprehension and retention, leading to a superficial grasp of concepts that quickly fade after the test.

Studies have shown that traditional teaching methods often result in lower levels of long-term retention and a weaker grasp of critical thinking skills. Students taught to focus primarily on test scores may prioritize short-term memorization over deep learning. This approach can lead to gaps in knowledge, where students remember facts for a test but need help understanding the underlying principles that connect those facts.

Moreover, emphasizing standardized testing can create a narrow focus in the curriculum, where teachers feel compelled to "teach to the test" rather than fostering a broader, more holistic understanding of the subject matter. This can limit students' exposure to diverse ideas, creative problem-solving, and interdisciplinary connections essential for success in the real world.

The data clearly show the impact of traditional teaching on academic outcomes. Students who are disengaged or emotionally disconnected from their learning often see a decline in their grades and test scores. This decline can create a vicious cycle, where poor performance leads to further disengagement, resulting in even lower academic achievement. The result is a growing number of students who, despite their potential, fall through the cracks of an educational system that needs to meet their needs.

A Call for Change: Teaching Differently Intentionally

The emotional and academic toll of traditional teaching methods indicates that the status quo needs to serve our students more effectively. While these methods may have been sufficient in the past, the demands of the modern world require a new approach to education—one that prioritizes students' emotional well-being, fosters deep and meaningful learning, and prepares them for the complexities of life beyond the classroom.

Teaching Differently Intentionally offers a pathway that recognizes the importance of addressing the whole student—emotionally, academically, and socially. By moving away from the limitations of traditional teaching and embracing a more flexible, student-centered approach, we can create learning environments where students thrive academically.

In the next chapter, we will explore how *Teaching Differently Intentionally* can be implemented in classrooms to counteract the adverse effects of traditional teaching and create a more positive, engaging, and practical educational experience for all students. The goal is to ensure that every student feels connected, valued, and equipped to succeed in an ever-changing world.

Chapter 4: A New Perspective: The Power of Intention in Teaching

Spark curiosity! Engaged students and an enthusiastic teacher showcase the magic of intentional teaching.

Chapter 4:
A New Perspective:
The Power of Intention in Teaching

Defining Intentional Teaching: Introduce the concept of teaching with intention and how it differs from traditional methods.

Benefits of Intentional Teaching: Highlight how this approach can improve student engagement, confidence, and academic success.

Chapter 4:
A New Perspective:
The Power of Intention in Teaching

Defining Intentional Teaching

In the ever-evolving landscape of education, the concept of *Teaching Differently Intentionally* emerges as a beacon of hope, offering a transformative shift from the traditional methods that have long dominated classrooms. At its core, intentional teaching is about purposefully designing and delivering lessons that meet the diverse needs of each student rather than adhering to a rigid, one-size-fits-all approach. It's about teaching with a clear vision, a deep understanding of each student's potential, and a commitment to nurturing that potential through deliberate, thoughtful actions.

Teaching Differently Intentionally is not just about changing how we teach; it's about changing the mindset behind teaching. It requires educators to move beyond the mechanics of instruction and engage in a more holistic, student-centered approach. This approach recognizes that every interaction, every lesson, and every moment in the classroom is an opportunity to inspire, challenge, and support students in their academic and personal growth. It is a shift from merely delivering content to facilitating meaningful learning experiences that resonate with students long after they leave the classroom.

This method starkly contrasts traditional teaching, which often focuses on covering the curriculum and preparing students for standardized tests. The conventional model emphasizes content delivery with little regard for how students absorb, process, and apply the information. In contrast, *Teaching Differently Intentionally* places the student at the center of the educational process. It encourages educators to be intentional in their planning, mindful of their instructional strategies, and reflective in their practice, always considering how their choices impact student learning and development.

Benefits of Intentional Teaching

The benefits of *Teaching Differently Intentionally* are profound and far-reaching. By shifting the focus to intentionality, educators can create environments that entice learning and empower students. When teachers approach their work intentionally, they are better equipped to connect with their students and understand their needs, strengths, and challenges. This deeper connection fosters a sense of trust and respect between the teacher and student, ensuring that the learning space is conducive to teaching and learning.

Improved Student Engagement

One of the most significant benefits of intentional teaching is the marked improvement in student engagement. When designed with intention, lessons are more likely to resonate with students, capturing their attention and actively engaging them in learning. Instead of sitting and getting information, students become active learners, eager to explore, question, and apply what they are learning. This heightened engagement leads to a more dynamic and interactive classroom where students feel valued and invested in their education.

Enhanced Confidence and Self-Efficacy

Another decisive outcome of *Teaching Differently Intentionally* is boosting student confidence and self-efficacy. When students feel that their individual needs and learning styles are being recognized and addressed, they eagerly participate in their learning and believe in their ability to succeed. This sense of confidence is further reinforced by the intentional use of formative assessments, personalized feedback, and opportunities for self-reflection, all of which help students see their progress and understand their strengths. As a result, they are more likely to take risks, persevere through challenges, and approach their learning with a growth mindset.

Academic Success and Beyond

Ultimately, the intentional approach to teaching leads to more tremendous academic success. By aligning instruction with students' unique needs and learning styles, educators can help students achieve more profound understanding and higher levels of mastery. However, the impact of *teaching differently intentionally* goes beyond test scores and grades. It prepares students for lifelong learning by equipping them with the critical thinking skills, problem-solving abilities, and resilience they need to navigate an increasingly complex world.

In addition to academic success, intentional teaching helps students develop the social-emotional skills crucial for success in life. By creating an inclusive, supportive classroom environment responsive to students' needs, educators can help students build strong relationships, manage their emotions, and develop a sense of purpose and direction.

Embracing a New Perspective

As we move forward in our journey of *Teaching Differently Intentionally*, it becomes clear that the power of intention in teaching is transformative. By embracing this new perspective, educators can comfortably reject the limitations of traditional methods and create learning experiences that are truly meaningful, relevant, and impactful.

The next chapter provides practical applications of *Teaching Differently Intentionally*, exploring strategies and techniques educators can use to bring intentionality into their classrooms. This method aims to navigate teachers beyond just teaching to inspiring, empowering, and guiding students toward a brighter future where they are eagerly prepared to share their knowledge, skills, and confidence to thrive on their chosen path.

Part Two: The Teaching Differently Intentionally Framework

The Teaching Differently Intentionally Framework
Chapter 5: Understanding the Framework

A visual roadmap: The "Teaching Differently Intentionally" framework, ready to guide educators.

This framework creates an engaging, student-centered environment where all students can succeed.

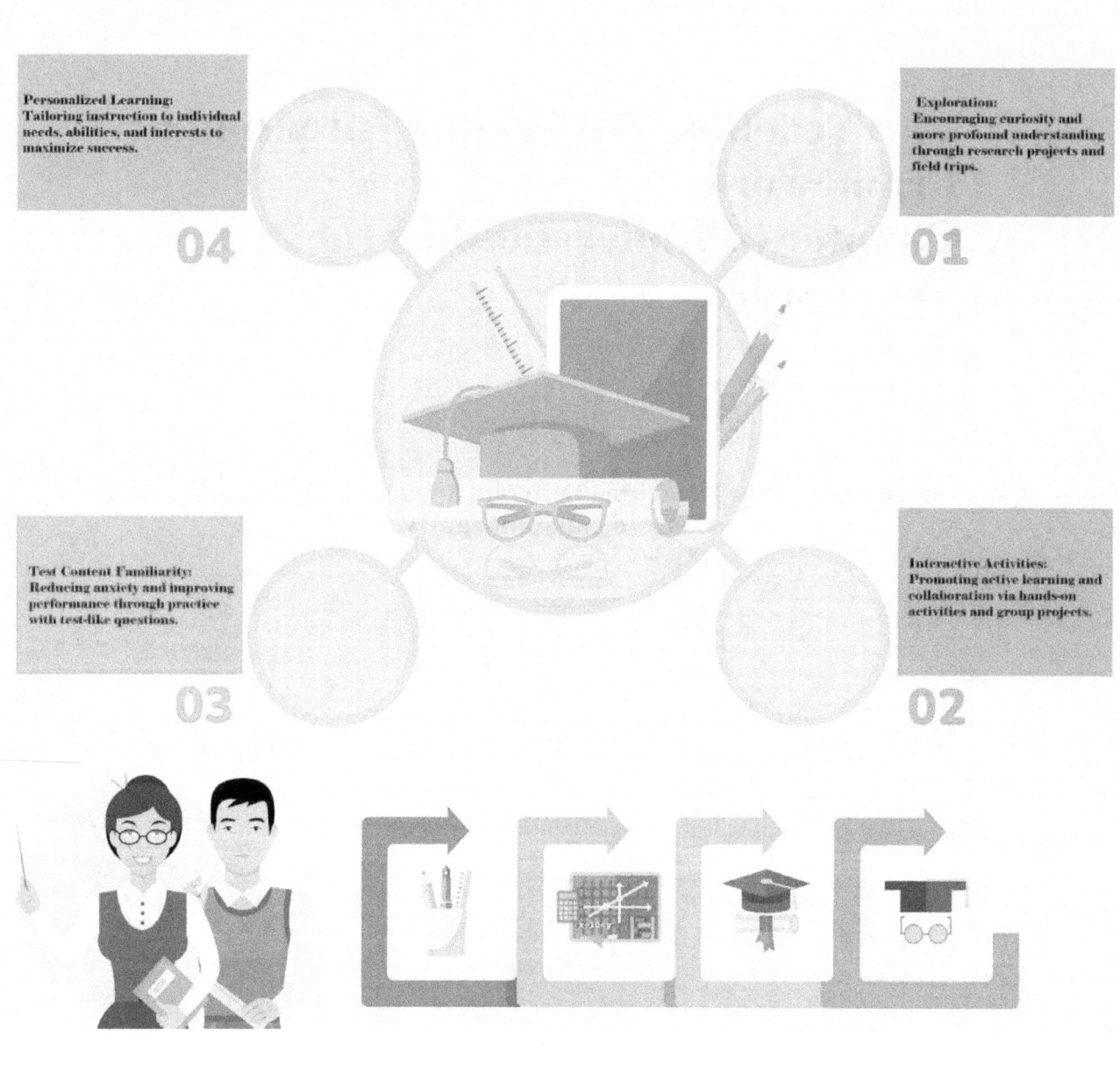

Personalized Learning: Tailoring instruction to individual needs, abilities, and interests to maximize success.

04

Exploration: Encouraging curiosity and more profound understanding through research projects and field trips.

01

Test Content Familiarity: Reducing anxiety and improving performance through practice with test-like questions.

03

Interactive Activities: Promoting active learning and collaboration via hands-on activities and group projects.

02

Chapter 5: Understanding the Framework

Overview of the Methodology: Provide a detailed explanation of the Teach Differently Intentionally framework, outlining its essential components and how it can be applied across various curricula.

Framework Components:

- Exploration
- Interactive Activities
- Test Content Familiarity
- Personalized Learning

Chapter 5:
Understanding the Framework

Overview of the Methodology

As educators, we understand that the future of teaching and learning lies not in tradition but in transformation. The *Teaching Differently Intentionally* framework is a revolutionary teaching method designed to meet the diverse needs of today's students and teachers. It is built on the belief that education should be a dynamic, personalized experience that fosters student-centered instruction, understanding, critical thinking, and a revived love of learning.

The *Teaching Differently Intentionally* framework is not a rigid set of instructions but a flexible, adaptable methodology that can be applied across various curricula. It empowers educators to move beyond the limitations of conventional teaching by providing them with the tools and strategies needed to create engaging, meaningful learning experiences. This framework is grounded in the idea that every student is unique, and therefore, teaching should be tailored to meet the individual needs of each learner.

This chapter will delve into the essential components of the *Teaching Differently Intentionally* framework. Each element fosters a holistic learning environment where students can thrive academically, emotionally, and socially. By understanding and implementing these components, educators can transform their teaching practices and, in turn, transform the lives of their students.

Framework Components

Exploration

At the heart of the *Teaching Differently Intentionally* framework is the principle of exploration. Traditional education often places students in a passive role, where they are expected to absorb information presented to them. In contrast, exploration invites students to participate actively in their learning. It encourages them to ask questions, investigate new ideas, and discover knowledge for themselves.

Exploration is about creating opportunities for students to engage with the material meaningfully. Through hands-on experiments, research projects, or real-world problem-solving, exploration allows students to connect their learning to their own experiences and interests. This makes learning more relevant, enjoyable, and memorable, and this teaching method helps students develop a deeper understanding and love for learning.

In the *Teaching Differently Intentionally* framework, exploration reveals the importance of explorational learning beyond the elementary years. It is a universal approach that can be integrated into any curriculum, encouraging students to become lifelong learners who are curious, interested, and eager to explore the world around them.

Interactive Activities

The second component of the *Teaching Differently Intentionally* framework is interactive activities. These activities are designed to make learning a collaborative and dynamic process where students actively participate rather than passively receive information. Interactive activities can take many forms, from group discussions and debates to role-playing, simulations, and hands-on experiments.

Interactive activities are essential because they engage students cognitively, socially, and emotionally on multiple levels. When students work together to solve problems, share ideas, or create something new, they create essential communication, collaboration, and empathy skills. Moreover, interactive activities help practically reinforce the material in a real-world context.

To enhance the impact of interactive activities, the *Teaching Differently Intentionally* framework encourages the integration of content into these activities. For example, after a lesson on historical events, students could participate in a debate in which they must defend different perspectives based on their understanding of the content. Alternatively, students might engage in a role-playing exercise in which they assume the identities of historical figures, deepening their comprehension through active participation.

Incorporating interactive activities into the classroom helps to break down the barriers that often exist in traditional education. It creates a more inclusive environment where students can contribute, learn from others, and feel valued. By making learning an active and engaging process, interactive activities help to foster a sense of community and belonging among students.

Test Content Familiarity

While exploration and interactive activities are crucial for fostering deep learning, the *Teaching Differently Intentionally* framework also recognizes the importance of preparing students for the realities of standardized testing. Test content familiarity is about ensuring that students are well-versed in the subject matter and comfortable with the format and expectations of the tests they will encounter.

In many cases, students struggle on standardized tests not because they lack knowledge but because they are unfamiliar with the test format or experience test anxiety. The *Teaching Differently Intentionally* framework addresses this by seamlessly and non-threateningly integrating test content familiarity into the curriculum.

A critical aspect of test content familiarity is the importance of reading explorations of texts. To build students' confidence and competence in handling test materials, the framework suggests incorporating at least two focused reading explorations into each unit of study. These reading explorations can involve analyzing passages similar to those found on standardized tests, discussing key themes, and identifying the types of questions that may be asked. By engaging with the text in a structured yet exploratory manner, students can develop the skills needed to navigate complex reading materials under test conditions.

In addition to reading explorations, practice tests and test-taking strategies are also integrated into the teaching process. These activities should familiarize students with the test format and enhance their analytical and critical thinking skills. For instance, students might practice breaking down complex questions, identifying distractors, and understanding the rationale behind correct answers. The goal is to build test content familiarity to reduce anxiety and boost confidence, allowing students to demonstrate their true abilities.

Personalized Learning

The final component of the *Teaching Differently Intentionally* framework is personalized learning. This approach acknowledges that no two students are alike; education should be tailored to meet each individual's unique needs, strengths, and interests. Personalized learning is about creating a flexible, student-centered environment where instruction is adapted to suit the learner rather than expecting the learner to adjust.

Personalized learning involves differentiating instruction based on students' learning styles, providing choices in how they engage with the material, and offering various pathways to achieving the same learning goals. It also includes providing individualized feedback and support, helping students set goals, and tracking their progress.

By embracing personalized learning, the *Teaching Differently Intentionally* framework ensures that all students have the opportunity to succeed. It empowers students to take ownership of their education, develop a sense of agency, and achieve their full potential.

A Framework for Transformation

The *Teaching Differently Intentionally* framework is more than just a set of strategies—it is a philosophy of education that seeks to transform how we teach and how students learn. Educators can create an engaging, inclusive, and empowering learning environment by incorporating exploration and interactive activities, test content familiarity through reading explorations, and personalized learning.

In the following chapters, we will explore how to implement each component in practice, providing educators with practical tools and examples to bring the *Teaching Differently Intentionally* framework to life. The journey of transformation begins with understanding the framework, and from here, we will move forward with the confidence and clarity needed to make a lasting impact on the lives of our students.

Notes:

Chapter 6: How Do You Learn? Survey

Students discover their unique learning styles, empowering teachers to personalize instruction.

Chapter 6:
How Do You Learn? Survey

Importance of Understanding Learning Styles: Discuss the importance of identifying students' preferred learning styles.

Implementation: Provide practical steps for administering the survey and using the results to tailor instruction.

Chapter 6: How Do You Learn? Survey

Importance of Understanding Learning Styles

One of the most transformative aspects of *Teaching Differently Intentionally* is recognizing that every student is unique, with their preferred ways of processing and understanding information. Understanding these learning styles is beneficial and guides the educator's decision-making process as they create accommodating learning styles that meet the needs of all students.

The Impact of Learning Styles on Education

Learning styles refer to how individuals prefer to learn and process information. Some students may excel when seeing information visually, through diagrams, charts, or written text. Others may learn best through auditory methods, such as listening to lectures or engaging in discussions. Still, others might be kinesthetic learners who need to touch, manipulate, or physically engage with the material to understand it fully.

When educators know their students' preferred learning styles, they can tailor their teaching methods to align with these preferences. This alignment not only enhances student engagement but also improves comprehension and retention. For instance, a visual learner might need help to grasp a concept if presented verbally. Still, they might excel when that information is conveyed through a diagram or visual representation.

Understanding learning styles is vital beyond academic performance. When students feel that their learning needs are recognized and respected, they are more likely to develop confidence in their abilities. This confidence fosters a positive attitude toward learning, which can impact their educational journey and beyond. By contrast, when students are consistently taught in ways that do not align with their learning styles, they may become frustrated, disengaged, and even develop a negative self-concept regarding their abilities.

Creating an Inclusive and Supportive Environment

Identifying and addressing different learning styles is crucial for creating an inclusive classroom environment. In a traditional classroom, where a single method of instruction is often used, students who need to align with that method may feel they need to be included or understood. This can lead to encouraging students to isolate and a lack of motivation to participate. By contrast, when teaching is differentiated to meet various learning styles, all students can succeed, fostering a sense of belonging and equity within the classroom.

Understanding learning styles also equips teachers with the knowledge to anticipate potential challenges and adapt their teaching strategies proactively. For example, if a teacher knows a student is a kinesthetic learner, they can incorporate more hands-on activities or movement-based learning opportunities into their lessons. Similarly, if teachers understand that a student is an auditory learner, they can ensure that oral instructions are clear and provide opportunities for verbal processing of information.

Implementation: Administering the How Do You Learn? Survey

The first step in tailoring instruction to meet students' diverse learning needs is to understand those needs. The *How Do You Learn? Survey* is a practical tool designed to help educators identify their students' preferred learning styles. Administering this survey is crucial in effectively implementing the *Teaching Differently Intentionally* framework.

Step 1: Administering the Survey

The *How Do You Learn? The survey* should be administered early in the school year or at the beginning of a new course. It is a simple, accessible tool that asks students questions about how they prefer to receive and process information. Depending on the resources available and the student's age, the survey can be conducted in various formats—paper-based, online, or even as an interactive classroom activity.

Explain to students the purpose of the survey and how the information will be used. Emphasize that there are no right or wrong answers and that the goal is to help them learn in the way that suits them best. This can help students feel more comfortable and honest in their responses.

Step 2: Analyzing the Results

Once the surveys are completed, the next step is to analyze the results. Look for patterns in the data to identify the predominant learning styles within the classroom. Some students strongly prefer one style, while others may have a more balanced approach, utilizing multiple styles depending on the situation.

Understanding the distribution of learning styles in your classroom is essential for planning lessons that engage all students. For example, suppose you discover that most of your students are visual learners. In that case, you might prioritize using visual aids, such as infographics or video content, in your instruction. However, ensuring that all learning styles are catered to is essential so students feel included.

Step 3: Tailoring Instruction

With the insights gained from the survey, you can begin to tailor your instruction to meet the needs of your students. This might involve incorporating a mix of teaching methods into your lessons. For instance:

- **Visual Learners:** Complement verbal instructions using diagrams, charts, and images. Encourage students to create mind maps or visual summaries of the material.
- **Auditory Learners:** Integrate more discussions, lectures, and oral presentations into your teaching. Allow students to record their ideas or participate in group discussions to reinforce learning.
- **Kinesthetic Learners:** Incorporate hands-on activities, experiments, or role-playing exercises that allow students to engage with the content physically. Consider incorporating movement into lessons, such as having students act out concepts or use gestures to represent ideas.

Step 4: Ongoing Reflection and Adjustment

Understanding and catering to learning styles is not a one-time activity but an ongoing process requiring regular reflection and adjustment. Throughout the school year, observe how students respond to different teaching methods. Are they more engaged when certain styles are used?

Are there any students who need help despite the accommodations? Use these observations to make necessary adjustments to your teaching strategies.

Additionally, consider administering the *How Do You Learn? Survey* again later in the year to see if students' preferences have evolved or new patterns have emerged. This ongoing assessment ensures that your teaching remains aligned with your student's needs, allowing you to continue providing a supportive and effective learning environment.

The Transformative Power of Understanding Learning Styles

By taking the time to understand how each student learns, you are not just enhancing their academic success—you are empowering them as learners and individuals. The *Teaching Differently Intentionally* framework strongly emphasizes the importance of this understanding, recognizing that it is critical to creating an educational experience that is inclusive, engaging, and deeply meaningful.

In the following chapters, we will explore how to integrate the insights gained from the *How Do You Learn? Survey* into specific instructional strategies and classroom activities. The transformation journey continues as we delve deeper into the practical applications of *Teaching Differently Intentionally*, ensuring that every student can and will learn.

Notes:

Chapter 7: Creating a Conducive Learning Environment

A vibrant, flexible classroom invites collaboration and exploration.

Create a flexible, adaptable classroom layout with diverse learning zones catering to visual, auditory, and kinesthetic learners.
In order to enhance interactive and exploratory learning, it's important to offer hands-on materials, educational technology, comfortable seating, and plenty of room for students to move around and work together.

Chapter 7:
Creating a Conducive Learning Environment

Classroom Dynamics: Explore how to design a classroom environment that supports diverse learning experiences.

Essential Tools: Discuss the materials and resources needed to create an interactive, exploratory learning space.

Chapter 7: Creating a Conducive Learning Environment

Classroom Dynamics

The environment in which students learn is as crucial as the content they are taught. A conducive learning environment is not just about the physical layout of the classroom; it's about creating a space that supports diverse learning experiences, fosters a sense of community, and encourages students to take ownership of their learning. The classroom dynamics play a pivotal role in the success of *Teaching Differently Intentionally*, as they set the tone for how students interact with the material, each other, and their teacher.

Designing for Flexibility and Inclusivity

One key aspect of *Teaching Differently Intentionally* is recognizing that students learn in different ways and at various paces. Therefore, the classroom environment must be flexible enough to accommodate these differences. Traditional rows of desks facing a blackboard or smartboard may be effective for some forms of instruction, but they can be limiting when fostering collaboration, exploration, and interactive learning.

Consider arranging the classroom to promote individual focus and group interaction to create a conducive learning environment. This might involve setting up different learning stations around the room, each tailored to a specific activity or learning style. For example, you might have a reading corner with comfortable seating for independent study, a collaborative area with round tables for group work, and a hands-on station with materials for experiments and creative projects.

It's also essential to ensure the classroom reveals its inclusivity and accessibility to each student. Providing alternative seating options, ensuring clear pathways for movement, and incorporating technology that supports diverse learning needs are all essential components of an inclusive classroom design.

Fostering a Sense of Community

Beyond the physical layout, the classroom dynamics should foster community and belonging among students. When students feel safe, respected, and valued, they are more likely to engage actively in their learning. This sense of community can be cultivated through various means, including how the classroom is decorated, the established norms and expectations, and the opportunities for students to share their ideas and collaborate.

Consider incorporating student work and achievements into the classroom decor. Displaying student projects, artwork, or other forms of expression personalizes the space and gives students the self-assurance needed to thrive in their learning environment. Additionally, creating a classroom culture that encourages open dialogue, mutual respect, and collaboration can help students feel more connected to one another and more invested in their learning.

Regularly involving students in the decision-making process—such as allowing them to choose some classroom rules or having a say in how specific lessons are structured—can also empower them and make them feel like active participants in their education. When students feel that their voices matter, they are more likely to engage deeply with the material and each other.

Essential Tools

Creating an environment that supports *Teaching Differently Intentionally* requires more than just the proper classroom layout—it also necessitates having the appropriate materials and resources. These resources and materials create an interactive, exploratory learning space that caters to students' diverse needs.

Interactive and Exploratory Materials

To foster exploration and interaction, the classroom should be equipped with various materials to encourage students to engage with the content in hands-on, meaningful ways. This might include:

- **Manipulatives:** These are physical objects that students can use to explore mathematical concepts, build models, or solve problems. Examples include blocks, counters, geometric shapes, or science kits. Manipulatives are particularly useful for kinesthetic learners who benefit from tactile experiences.

- **Visual Aids:** Charts, diagrams, posters, and other visual tools, such as Interactive whiteboards or smartboards, to display dynamic content, such as videos or interactive simulations, which can engage visual learners.
- **Technology:** Technology use in the classroom can enhance the learning experience for all students. Cellphones, Tablets, laptops, and educational software can provide interactive learning opportunities, while online resources can offer access to a wealth of information and activities that complement the curriculum.
- **Art Supplies:** A well-stocked supply of art materials (such as paper, paints, markers, and clay) can be invaluable for creative projects or when exploring concepts through artistic expression. These supplies enable students to express their understanding in diverse and personalized ways.
- **Reading Materials:** A well-curated library of print-rich/digital books, magazines, and articles covering student interests and reading levels is essential. This allows students to explore exciting subjects and practice reading skills in a relevant and engaging context.

Creating Zones for Different Learning Activities

In addition to having suitable materials, organizing the classroom into distinct zones can help facilitate different learning activities. These zones should be clearly defined and equipped with the necessary resources to support their intended purpose. Some examples of learning zones might include:

- **Reading Zone:** A quiet, comfortable area where students can engage in independent reading or small group discussions. This zone might include soft seating, bookshelves, and reading lamps to create a cozy, inviting atmosphere.
- **Collaboration Zone:** A space designed for group work where students can brainstorm, discuss ideas, and work on projects together. This area might feature round tables, whiteboards, and supplies for note-taking or drawing.
- **Exploration Zone:** A hands-on area with materials for experiments, construction, or artistic creation. This zone should have manipulatives, art supplies, science kits, or other resources that encourage active exploration and problem-solving.

- **Technology Zone:** A classroom section dedicated to digital learning, where students can use computers, tablets, or other technological tools to access online resources, complete assignments, or collaborate on digital projects.

Flexible and Adaptive Furniture

To support the dynamic nature of *Teaching Differently Intentionally*, it's essential to have relevant student-centered furniture that easily adjusts to accommodate different learning activities. This might include:

- **Movable Desks and Chairs:** Furniture that can be easily moved allows for quick reconfiguration of the classroom layout to suit different activities, whether it's a group discussion, individual work, or a collaborative project.
- **Standing Desks or Adjustable Tables:** Providing various seating options, including standing desks or adjustable tables, can help meet the needs of different students, particularly those who may benefit from changing positions throughout the day.
- **Storage Solutions:** Adequate storage for materials and resources ensures that everything is organized and accessible. This might include shelves, bins, or carts that can quickly move around the classroom.

Building a Conducive Learning Environment

Creating a conducive learning environment is about more than just the physical space; it's about fostering a dynamic, inclusive atmosphere that supports the diverse learning needs of all students. By thoughtfully considering the classroom layout, tools, and resources, educators can create a space that enhances learning and makes students feel valued, respected, and engaged.

In the following chapters, we will explore how to implement the *Teaching Differently Intentionally* framework within this conducive learning environment, ensuring that every student has the opportunity to succeed. Educators create classrooms where all students thrive by combining intentional design with thoughtful instruction.

Notes:

Chapter 8: Start with the Test Content

Confident students tackle practice tests, building familiarity and easing anxiety.

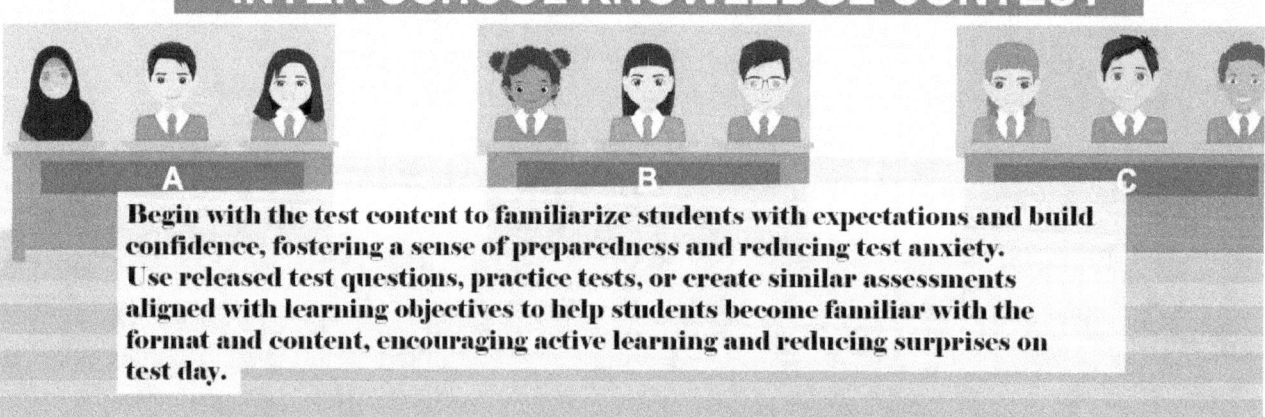

Begin with the test content to familiarize students with expectations and build confidence, fostering a sense of preparedness and reducing test anxiety. Use released test questions, practice tests, or create similar assessments aligned with learning objectives to help students become familiar with the format and content, encouraging active learning and reducing surprises on test day.

Chapter 8:
Start with the Test Content

Reverse Engineering Learning: Explain the concept of starting with the test content and how it helps students build familiarity and confidence.

Practical Application: Provide examples of implementing this approach in the classroom.

Chapter 8:
Start with the Test Content

Reverse Engineering Learning

In education, preparing students for assessments has traditionally involved teaching the material first and then introducing the test content as a final step. However, the *Teaching Differently Intentionally* framework advocates for a different approach that begins with the end in mind. This method, reverse engineering learning, starts with the test content and works backward to build lessons and activities that align with the knowledge and skills students need to succeed.

The Power of Starting with Test Content

Reverse engineering learning is based on the principle that familiarity with test content can significantly boost students' confidence and performance. When students are introduced to the types of questions, formats, and expectations they will encounter on assessments early in the learning process, they become more comfortable with the test. This familiarity reduces anxiety, demystifies the testing process, and allows students to focus on mastering the content rather than being overwhelmed by the format.

By starting with the test content, educators can ensure that their lessons are directly aligned with the objectives and skills that will be assessed. This alignment improves the instruction's relevance and helps students see the direct connection between what they are learning and how it will be evaluated. Rather than viewing the test as a separate, intimidating hurdle, students understand it as an integrated part of their learning journey.

Reverse engineering also provides a clear roadmap for instruction. Educators can design their lessons to systematically build the knowledge and competencies needed for success by identifying the key concepts and skills to be assessed. This approach ensures that no critical areas are overlooked and that students are fully prepared for the test's content and structure.

Practical Application

Implementing reverse engineering learning in the classroom involves a strategic approach to lesson planning and instruction. Here are some practical examples of how this method can be applied across different subjects:

Example 1: Preparing for a History Exam

Imagine a history teacher who knows that the upcoming exam will focus on significant events of the American Revolution, including critical battles, influential figures, and the war's impact on various groups. Instead of starting with broad lessons on the Revolution and then narrowing down to the test content, the teacher introduces students to sample test questions and prompts.

For instance, the teacher might present a typical test question, "Describe the significance of the Battle of Saratoga in the context of the American Revolution." Students would then engage in activities designed to build their understanding of this event, such as analyzing primary source documents, participating in debates about the battle's outcomes, or creating timelines that place the event in a broader historical context.

The teacher continually revisits the test content throughout the unit, using practice questions and discussions to reinforce critical concepts. By the time the actual exam arrives, students are not only familiar with the content but also comfortable with the format and expectations of the test.

Example 2: Math and Problem-Solving

In a math classroom, the teacher knows that the final assessment will include word problems requiring the application of specific mathematical concepts, such as algebraic equations or geometry principles. Rather than teaching the math concepts in isolation and introducing word problems as an afterthought, the teacher starts with sample word problems similar to those on the test.

At the beginning of the unit, students are asked to attempt these problems, even if they haven't mastered the necessary skills. This initial exposure helps students identify the types of thinking and strategies required to solve these problems. The teacher then uses this insight to guide the instruction, building students' specific skills and knowledge to approach these problems confidently.

Throughout the unit, the teacher incorporates regular practice with similar problems, gradually increasing complexity as students develop skills. By reaching the final assessment, students can solve the issues and be familiar with the test format, reducing test-related anxiety.

Example 3: Language Arts and Analytical Writing

In a language arts class, students prepare for an assessment that includes essay writing and literary analysis. The teacher begins the unit by showing students examples of high-scoring essays and analysis questions similar to the tests. Students analyze these examples, discussing their effectiveness and how they address the prompts.

Based on this analysis, the teacher develops lessons on the skills required to produce similar work, such as thesis development, textual evidence integration, and cohesive argumentation. Students practice writing their essays and receive feedback aligned with the criteria used in the test.

As students progress, they are given opportunities to revise their work based on the feedback, with each iteration bringing them closer to the level of proficiency required for the test. By the end of the unit, students have developed strong analytical and writing skills and a clear understanding of how to apply these skills in the test context.

The Benefits of Reverse Engineering Learning

The reverse engineering approach, where instruction begins with the test content, offers several key benefits:

1. **Increased Familiarity:** Students become accustomed to the types of questions and formats they encounter on assessments, reducing anxiety and building confidence.

2. **Targeted Instruction:** By aligning lessons with the skills and knowledge required for the test, educators can ensure that their teaching is focused and relevant.

3. **Improved Performance:** When students understand the expectations and have ample practice with the test content, they are likelier to perform well, demonstrating their proper understanding of the material.

4. **Greater Student Engagement:** Students who see the direct connection between their learning and how they will be assessed stay motivated and engaged throughout the learning process.

Integrating Reverse Engineering Learning into Your Teaching

To successfully integrate reverse engineering learning into your classroom, consider the following steps:

- **Start with the End in Mind:** Begin your lesson planning by reviewing the test content and identifying the essential skills and knowledge to be assessed. Use this information to design your lessons, ensuring each activity aligns with the test objectives.
- **Introduce Test Content Early:** Present sample test questions, prompts, or problems at the beginning of the unit to give students a sense of what to expect. Use these samples as a basis for discussion and analysis, helping students understand the criteria for success.
- **Build Skills Gradually:** Use the test content as a guide for scaffolding instruction. Start with foundational skills and gradually increase the complexity of the tasks as students' proficiency grows.
- **Provide Ongoing Practice:** Regularly incorporate practice with test-like questions and formats throughout the unit. Use these opportunities to provide feedback and guide students toward improvement.
- **Reflect and Adjust:** After each assessment, reflect on how well the reverse engineering approach worked. Use this reflection to adjust your instruction and better meet the needs of your students in future units.

By starting with the test content and using it as a foundation for your instruction, you can help students build the familiarity, confidence, and skills they need to succeed. This approach prepares students for assessments and transforms how they engage with the material, making learning a more intentional, meaningful, and empowering experience.

Notes:

Part Three: Strategies for Engagement and Success

Strategies for Engagement and Success
Chapter 9: Interactive Activities for Memorable Learning

Hands-on projects and real-world connections make learning fun and unforgettable.

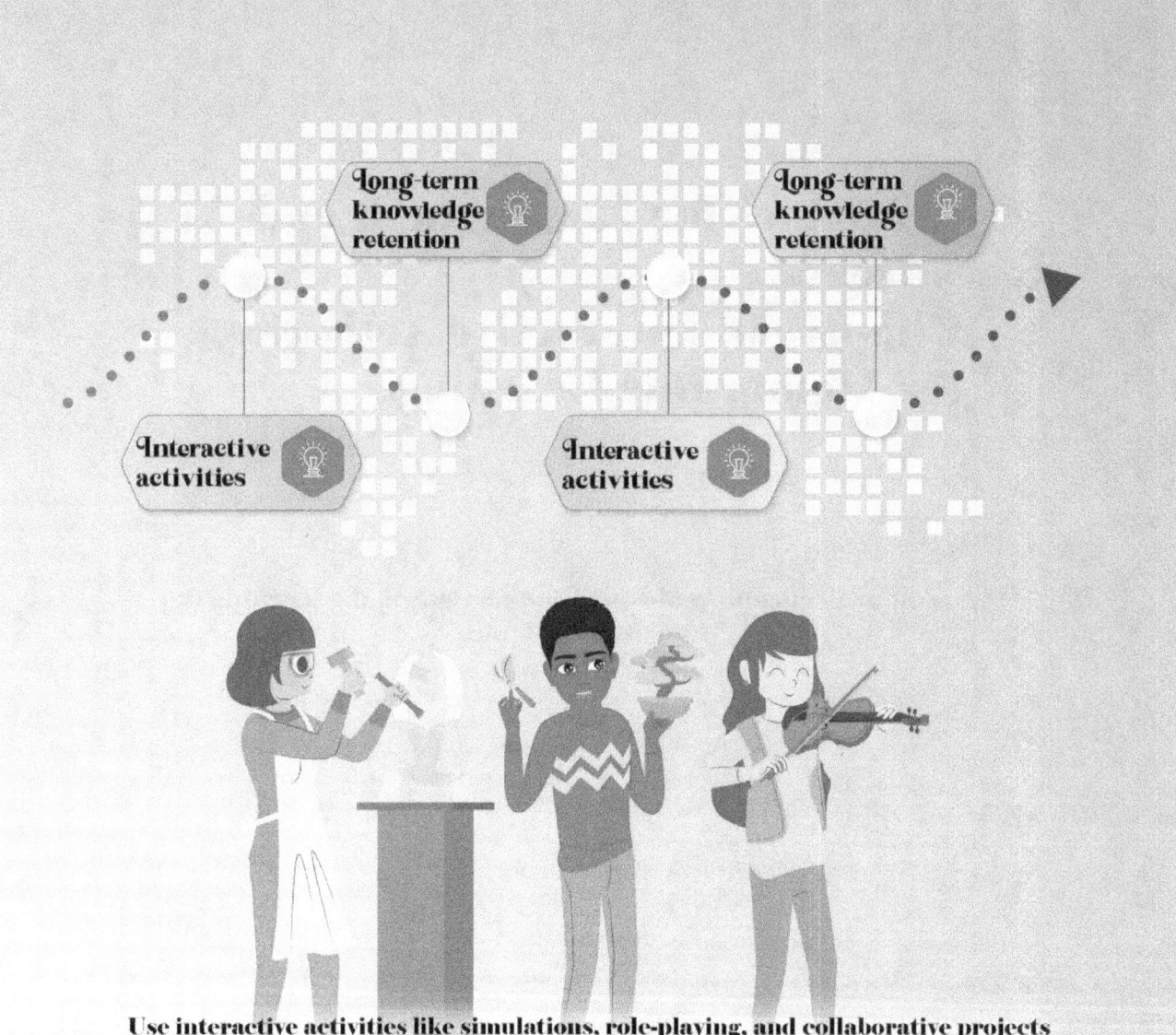

Use interactive activities like simulations, role-playing, and collaborative projects to make learning more memorable and engaging and foster deeper understanding and retention.
Link learning to real-world applications and current events to enhance relevance and retention. This will allow students to see the practical value of their knowledge and skills, ultimately motivating them to learn more.

Chapter 9:
Interactive Activities for Memorable Learning

Engagement Techniques: Explore various interactive activities that make learning memorable and engaging.

Real-World Connections: Discuss the importance of linking learning to real-world situations and how it enhances retention.

Chapter 9:
Interactive Activities for Memorable Learning

Engagement Techniques

Creating memorable learning experiences is at the heart of the *Teaching Differently Intentionally* framework. One of the most effective ways to make learning stick is through interactive activities that actively engage students in discovery and application. These activities transform the classroom from a passive environment into a dynamic space where students are encouraged to explore, collaborate, and think critically. This chapter will explore various engagement techniques that make learning memorable and enjoyable.

The Power of Interactive Learning

Interactive learning is more than just an instructional strategy; it is a philosophy that places students at the center of their education. Students must actively participate in the learning process, and teachers ensure they do so by fostering more profound understanding, excellent retention, and a more positive attitude toward instruction and learning. Interactive activities cater to different learning styles and make abstract concepts more concrete and accessible.

Moreover, interactive learning taps into students' natural curiosity and creativity. Students become more invested in learning When they can experiment, solve problems, and collaborate with their peers. This investment leads to greater motivation, a critical factor in academic success.

Techniques for Effective Interactive Activities

1. **Think-Pair-Share:**

    How It Works: Students think individually about a question or problem the teacher poses. Afterward, they paired up with a classmate to discuss their thoughts and ideas before sharing their insights with the larger group.

Why It's Effective: This technique encourages individual reflection, peer collaboration, and public speaking. It also allows students to articulate their thoughts and learn from others, deepening their understanding of the topic.

2. **Role-Playing:**

   How It Works: Students take on roles related to the studied content, such as historical figures, characters from a story, or professionals in a particular field. They act out scenarios that allow them to explore different perspectives and make decisions based on their roles.

   Why It's Effective: Role-playing makes learning more relatable and helps students empathize with different viewpoints. It also encourages creativity, critical thinking, and communication skills.

3. **Problem-Based Learning (PBL):**

   How It Works: Students are presented with a real-world problem and work in groups to research, analyze, and propose solutions. The teacher is a facilitator, guiding students through the process rather than providing direct answers.

   Why It's Effective: PBL promotes deep learning by requiring students to apply their knowledge to real-world situations. It also enhances collaboration, research skills, and the ability to synthesize information.

4. **Gamification:**

   How It Works: Teachers incorporate game-like elements into the classroom, such as points, badges, leaderboards, and challenges. These elements can motivate students, reinforce learning, and make the classroom experience more enjoyable.

   Why It's Effective: Gamification leverages the intrinsic motivation of play. It can make learning fun and competitive, encouraging students to push themselves further and engage more deeply with the content.

5. **Debates:**

   How It Works: Students are divided into groups and assigned different positions on a controversial issue related to the subject matter. They must research their position, develop arguments, and engage in a structured debate with the opposing side.

Why It's Effective: Debates encourage critical thinking, public speaking, and the ability to construct and defend an argument. They also help students understand multiple perspectives on an issue, promoting empathy and open-mindedness.

6. **Interactive Simulations:**

How It Works: Students use digital or physical simulations that mimic real-world processes or scenarios. For example, they might participate in a stock market simulation, a science lab experiment, or a historical reenactment.
Why It's Effective: Simulations provide a hands-on experience that can make complex concepts more understandable. They also allow students to experiment with different outcomes and see the immediate consequences of their decisions.

7. **Jigsaw Activities:**

How It Works: A topic is divided into several segments, and students are assigned to become "experts" on one segment. They then teach their segment to their peers, piecing together the entire topic.
Why It's Effective: Jigsaw activities promote collaborative learning and ensure that every student contributes to the group's understanding. It also reinforces the idea that learning is a shared responsibility.

Real-World Connections

While interactive activities are powerful tools for engagement, their impact is magnified when connected to real-world situations. Making learning relevant to students' lives helps them see the value in their studies and understand how it applies beyond the classroom.

The Importance of Real-World Relevance

Linking classroom content to real-world situations enhances retention by providing context and meaning to the material. When students can relate what they are learning to their own experiences, they are more likely to remember and apply the knowledge. This relevance also helps to bridge the gap between theory and practice, showing students that what they learn in school has practical applications in the world around them.

Real-world connections also make learning more engaging. Students are naturally more interested in topics that directly impact their lives or that they can see in action outside of the classroom. By tying lessons to current events, community issues, or future career paths, teachers can capture students' interests and make learning more dynamic and impactful.

Techniques for Making Real-World Connections

1. **Case Studies:**

   How It Works: Present students with authentic, real-world case studies or scenarios that require them to apply the concepts they have learned. These could be based on events, business situations, scientific discoveries, or social issues.

   Why It's Effective: Case studies provide a concrete context for abstract concepts and encourage students to think critically about how to apply their knowledge in real situations.

2. **Field Trips and Guest Speakers:**

   How It Works: Organize field trips to locations relevant to the subject, such as museums, businesses, or natural sites. Alternatively, invite guest speakers who are lively and energetic experts in the field to share their experiences and insights with students.

   Why It's Effective: Field trips and guest speakers provide firsthand experiences and bring the curriculum to life. They allow students to see the real-world applications of what they are learning and connect with professionals in the field.

3. **Service Learning Projects:**

   How It Works: Integrate community service projects into the curriculum that address real-world problems. Students can apply their knowledge to positively impact their community through environmental initiatives, social justice campaigns, or health awareness programs.

   Why It's Effective: Service learning gives students a sense of purpose and agency, showing them that their education can be used to effect change in the world. It also helps develop empathy, civic responsibility, and leadership skills.

4. **Current Events Integration:**

   How It Works: Incorporate current events into lessons by discussing recent news stories, social trends, or technological advancements related to the subject matter. Encourage students to analyze how these events impact their lives and society.

   Why It's Effective: Connecting lessons to current events makes learning timely and relevant. It teaches students the importance of staying informed and allows them to apply their critical thinking skills to real-world issues.

5. **Project-Based Learning (PBL):**

   How It Works: Develop projects that require students to solve real-world problems or create products that have practical applications. For example, students might design a sustainable energy solution, develop a business plan, or create a public awareness campaign.

   Why It's Effective: PBL engages students in deep learning by requiring them to apply their knowledge meaningfully. This learning strategy increases essential learning skills such as collaboration, time management, and problem-solving.

6. **Career Connections:**

   How It Works: Relate the content taught to potential career paths and industries. For example, if teaching mathematics, discuss how different professions (e.g., engineering, finance, architecture) use the math concepts being learned.

   Why It's Effective: Connecting lessons to careers helps students understand the practical applications of their education and can motivate them by showing the potential for future opportunities. It also helps them make informed decisions about their academic and professional futures.

The Transformative Power of Interactive and Real-World Learning

Interactive activities and real-world connections are powerful tools within the *Teaching Differently Intentionally* framework. They make learning memorable by engaging students on multiple levels—cognitively, emotionally, and socially. These techniques help students retain information and understand why and how the content is used in the broader context of their lives.

In the forthcoming chapters, we will continue exploring how these educational principles can be integrated into various academic subjects, providing educators with practical strategies to make learning meaningful and impactful. By embracing interactive and real-world learning, teachers create educational experiences that grant students opportunities to apply their knowledge and skills in the world beyond the classroom.

Notes:

Chapter 10: Continuous Progress Monitoring

Personalized feedback empowers students to take ownership of their growth.

Importance of Ongoing Assessment: Regular assessment enables tailored instruction and timely feedback for improved learning.
Tools and Techniques: Utilize formative and summative assessments, rubrics, and self-assessments to gather data and provide feedback, guiding student learning and promoting growth.

Chapter 10:
Continuous Progress Monitoring

Importance of Ongoing Assessment: Explain the significance of regularly assessing student progress and providing feedback.

Tools and Techniques: Provide various tools and techniques for effective progress monitoring.

Chapter 10: Continuous Progress Monitoring

Importance of Ongoing Assessment

In the education journey, progress is not a destination but a continuous growth, reflection, and improvement process. The *Teaching Differently Intentionally* framework emphasizes the importance of continuous progress monitoring as a vital component of effective teaching. Regularly assessing student progress and providing timely feedback are essential practices that ensure students stay on track toward their learning goals while allowing educators to adapt their teaching strategies to meet their students' evolving needs.

The Role of Continuous Assessment in Student Success

Continuous progress monitoring is more than just an occasional check-in or a final grade at the end of a unit; it is an ongoing process that provides real-time insights into student learning. By regularly assessing student progress, educators can identify strengths, areas for improvement, and potential challenges before they become significant obstacles. This proactive approach allows for timely interventions that substantially impact a student's academic journey.

Ongoing assessment helps students stay engaged and motivated by providing them with a clear understanding of their progress. When students receive regular feedback, they are more likely to take ownership of their learning, set personal goals, and strive to improve. This sense of accountability fosters a growth mindset, where students view challenges as opportunities to learn and develop rather than as setbacks.

Moreover, continuous progress monitoring ensures that instruction remains aligned with student needs. It allows educators to adjust their teaching strategies in response to the data they collect, ensuring that all students receive the support and guidance they need to succeed. This adaptability is crucial in creating a learning environment that intentionally drives students to reach their full potential.

Benefits of Continuous Progress Monitoring

1. **Personalized Learning:** Continuous assessment provides insights into each student's unique learning needs, enabling educators to tailor their instruction to better meet those needs. This customized approach ensures that all students receive the appropriate level of challenge and support.
2. **Early Intervention:** By monitoring progress regularly, educators can identify potential learning difficulties early on. This allows for timely interventions that prevent minor issues from becoming significant barriers to success.
3. **Increased Student Engagement:** Regular feedback keeps students updated on their understanding of the concept being taught, helping them stay motivated and engaged. It also encourages a sense of responsibility and ownership over their learning journey.
4. **Informed Decision-Making:** Continuous progress monitoring provides educators with the data they need to make informed decisions about instruction, curriculum pacing, and resource allocation. This data-driven approach ensures that teaching is effective and responsive to student needs.
5. **Fostering a Growth Mindset:** When students see that their progress is being tracked and that they are receiving feedback aimed at helping them improve, they adopt a growth mindset. This mindset encourages resilience, perseverance, and a positive attitude toward learning.

Tools and Techniques for Effective Progress Monitoring

Implementing continuous progress monitoring requires the right tools and techniques to collect, analyze, and respond to student data. Here are some effective methods that can be integrated into the classroom:

1. Formative Assessments

Formative assessments are low-stakes evaluations that provide immediate feedback on student learning. Teachers evaluate student learning at the end of an instructional period or unit using summative declaration, project, etc; formative assessments are conducted regularly throughout the learning process.

- **Exit Tickets:** At the end of a lesson, students complete a quick assessment (such as answering a question or summarizing what they learned) before leaving the classroom. This provides the teacher immediate feedback on student understanding and highlights areas needing further clarification.
- **Quizzes:** Short quizzes can be administered periodically to assess student comprehension of recently covered material. These quizzes can be graded or ungraded, and their primary purpose is to gauge understanding and identify areas for review.
- **Think-Alouds:** During problem-solving or reading activities, students verbalize their thought processes. This technique allows teachers to assess how students approach tasks and identify misconceptions or gaps in understanding.
- **Peer Assessments:** Students use a rubric or checklist to assess each other's work. This provides additional feedback and helps students develop critical thinking and evaluative skills.

2. Performance-Based Assessments

Performance-based assessments require students to demonstrate their knowledge and skills through real-world tasks or projects. These assessments are practical for monitoring progress in applied learning and higher-order thinking skills.

- **Project-Based Learning (PBL):** Students work on long-term projects to reveal what they have learned to solve real-world problems. Educators can monitor progress throughout the project through checkpoints, drafts, and peer reviews.
- **Portfolios:** Students compile a collection of their work over time, showcasing their progress and achievements. Portfolios share evidence of the student's learning journey/process and provide teachers with a comprehensive view of student growth.
- **Presentations and Demonstrations:** Students present their work or demonstrate their understanding of a concept to the class. This allows teachers to assess content knowledge and communication and presentation skills.

3. Observation and Anecdotal Records

Observation is a powerful tool for progress monitoring, especially for assessing student behavior, engagement, and social interactions. By observing students in different contexts, educators can gain insights into areas that traditional assessments may need to capture.

- **Anecdotal Records:** Teachers keep brief, descriptive notes on student behavior, participation, and interactions during class activities. These records can highlight patterns or changes in student performance and inform instructional adjustments.
- **Checklists:** Teachers use checklists to track specific behaviors, skills, or milestones students are expected to achieve. Checklists provide a clear and organized way to monitor progress over time.

4. Technology-Based Assessments

Technology can significantly enhance progress monitoring by providing instant feedback, data analysis, and personalized learning experiences. Various digital tools and platforms offer innovative ways to assess and track student progress.

- **Learning Management Systems (LMS):** Platforms like Google Classroom, Canvas, or Moodle allow teachers to assign, grade, and track student work online. These systems often include analytics features that provide student performance and engagement insights.
- **Adaptive Learning Software:** Programs like Khan Academy or IXL adapt to each student's learning level, offering personalized practice and assessments. These tools provide immediate feedback and track progress, making it easier for teachers to identify strengths and areas for improvement.
- **Digital Portfolios:** Students create digital portfolios using Seesaw or Google Sites. These portfolios allow students to showcase their work, provide reflection time, and receive feedback from teachers and peers.

5. Self-Assessment and Reflection

Students are expected to assess their progress and reflect on their learning. Self-assessment fosters a sense of ownership and helps students develop critical thinking and self-regulation skills.

- **Learning Journals:** Students keep journals where they regularly reflect on what they have learned, challenges they faced, and goals they have set for themselves. Teachers can review these journals to gain insights into student progress and provide targeted feedback.

- **Rubrics and Checklists:** Provide students with rubrics or checklists that outline the criteria for success in a given task. Students can use these tools to assess their work before submitting it for teacher evaluation.
- **Goal-Setting Conferences:** Periodically, hold one-on-one conferences with students to review their progress, discuss their goals, and set new objectives. These conferences provide an opportunity for personalized attention to their learning targets.

The Transformative Impact of Continuous Progress Monitoring

Continuous progress monitoring is a cornerstone of the *Teaching Differently Intentionally* framework. It ensures that teaching is responsive, students are supported, and learning is a dynamic, evolving process. By regularly assessing student progress and providing timely feedback, educators can create a classroom environment where every student has the opportunity to succeed.

In the following chapters, we will explore how to integrate these tools and techniques into daily classroom practice, ensuring that progress monitoring becomes culturally embedded into the learning experience. By embracing continuous progress monitoring, educators empower students to take charge of their learning, foster a culture of growth and improvement, and ultimately achieve tremendous academic success.

Chapter 11: Presenting Learning in Their Own Way

Creativity unleashed! Students showcase their knowledge through diverse projects.

Chapter 11:
Presenting Learning in Their Way

Student-Centered Learning: Discuss the benefits of allowing students to demonstrate their knowledge in ways that suit their strengths and interests.

Rubric-Based Assessment: Explain how to use rubrics to evaluate student projects while encouraging creativity and ownership.

Chapter 11:
Presenting Learning in Their Way

Student-Centered Learning: Demonstrating Knowledge in Diverse Ways

Student-centered learning recognizes students as unique individuals with varying strengths, interests, and learning styles. Educators have created an inclusive and engaging classroom environment where students demonstrate their knowledge in ways that resonate with them. This approach goes beyond traditional assessment methods, such as paper-and-pencil tests, to encompass a broader range of skills and abilities. When students can choose how they express their understanding, they are more likely to develop a deeper connection to the material, fostering critical thinking, problem-solving, and creativity. Moreover, offering multiple pathways to demonstrate learning accommodates diverse learners, ensuring that all students have opportunities to succeed and shine.

By giving students agency in presenting their knowledge, educators empower them to embrace their learning and fully believe in their abilities. This approach aligns with the demands of the 21st century, where adaptability, innovation, and communication are essential skills.

Benefits of Student-Centered Learning:

- **Increased Motivation:** When students have choices in demonstrating their learning, they are more likely to demonstrate motivation and engagement in their learning process.
- **Enhanced Creativity:** Allowing students to express their knowledge through various mediums encourages innovative thinking and problem-solving skills.
- **Deeper Understanding:** Students who can choose how to present their learning often develop a more profound comprehension of the material as they connect it to their interests.
- **Differentiation:** By offering multiple pathways for demonstrating knowledge, educators can better accommodate the diverse learning styles and abilities within the classroom.
- **Skill Development:** Students develop essential 21st-century skills such as communication, collaboration, and presentation abilities.

Strategies for Implementing Student-Centered Learning:

- **Offer a Variety of Assessment Options:** Provide students with various choices for demonstrating their understanding, such as written reports, presentations, multimedia projects, performances, or portfolios.
- **Incorporate Student Interests:** Allow students to select topics or projects that align with their passions, enabling them to delve deeper into subjects that interest them.
- **Provide Clear Expectations:** While offering choices, it is essential to establish clear learning objectives and expectations for each assessment option.
- **Foster Collaboration:** Intentionally allow students to collaborate on projects and engage in teamwork and peer learning.
- **Provide Feedback:** Intentionally offer feedback that focuses on the student's strengths and areas for growth, helping them to improve their work.

Rubric-Based Assessment: Encouraging Creativity and Ownership

Create Rubrics written with precision that provide clear criteria for evaluating student work. They can promote creativity and ownership when used effectively while ensuring students meet learning objectives.

Critical Components of a Rubric:

- **Performance Levels:** Define different levels of achievement, such as exemplary, proficient, developing, and beginning.
- **Criteria:** Clearly outline the specific skills, knowledge, or qualities that will be assessed.
- **Descriptors:** Provide detailed descriptions of what each performance level looks like for each criterion.

Using Rubrics to Encourage Creativity and Ownership:

- **Focus on Process and Product:** Evaluate not only the final product but also the student's process, including their creativity, problem-solving, and perseverance.
- **Provide Choice:** Offer students options within the rubric to demonstrate their understanding in various ways.

- **Use Student Language:** Involve students in developing the rubric to increase ownership and engagement.
- **Offer Descriptive Feedback:** Provide intentional constructive input that deepens students' understanding of their strengths and areas for improvement.
- **Celebrate Growth:** Emphasize progress over perfection, fostering a positive learning environment.

Educators can create a classroom culture that values creativity, critical thinking, and individual expression by implementing student-centered learning and effectively utilizing rubrics.

Unleashing Student Potential: Diverse Paths to Learning

Examples of Student Projects:

- **History:** Instead of a traditional research paper, students can create a historical digital documentary, design a museum exhibit, or write or create a digital historical fiction novel.
- **Science:** Students can construct a model, experiment, create a science-themed comic book, or develop a public service announcement about a scientific issue.
- **English Language Arts:** Students can write poetry, create a short film based on a literary work, design a character analysis website, or perform a dramatic scene interpretation.
- **Math:** Students can create a math-themed board game, develop a real-world application of a mathematical concept, or create a visual representation of a mathematical problem.

Example of Student Choice:

In a unit on the American Revolution, students could choose from the following assessment options:

- Write, Type, or Video Record (reading) a persuasive essay arguing for or against the American Revolution.
- Create a timeline or infographic illustrating key events and figures.
- Design a board game that simulates the major battles of the war.
- Write and perform a play about a significant event or person from the Revolution.

Rubric-Based Assessment: Encouraging Creativity and Ownership

Example Rubric Criteria for a History Project:

Performance Level	Understanding of Historical Context	Creativity and Originality	Presentation Quality
Exemplary	Demonstrates a deep understanding of historical events and figures	Presents a unique and innovative perspective	The project is visually appealing, well-organized, and engaging
Proficient	Demonstrates a solid understanding of historical events and figures	Shows evidence of creative thinking	The project is well-presented and easy to follow
Developing	Demonstrates a basic knowledge of historical events and figures	Shows some effort at creativity	The project is somewhat organized but lacks visual appeal
Beginning	Demonstrates limited understanding of historical events and figures	Lacks creativity and originality	The project is poorly organized and difficult to follow

Example of Student Involvement in Rubric Creation:

In a science unit on ecosystems, students can help develop the rubric by identifying the critical elements of a thriving ecosystem project. They suggest criteria such as accuracy of scientific information, creativity in project design, effectiveness of communication, and teamwork collaboration.

Example of Descriptive Feedback:

Instead of saying, "Good job," a teacher might provide feedback like: "Your historical analysis of the causes of the Civil War was insightful. You effectively used primary sources to support your arguments. To strengthen your project, consider exploring the perspectives of different groups affected by the war."

By offering diverse assessment options, involving students in the rubric creation process, and providing specific and constructive feedback, educators can foster a classroom environment where students facilitate ownership of their learning and showcase their talents creatively and meaningfully.

Notes:

Part Four: Implementing and Reflecting

Implementing and Reflecting Chapter 12: Testing the Learning Process

Practice makes progress. Students use quizzes to reflect and refine their understanding.

Practice tests and quizzes familiarize students with the format and content of real assessments, reducing anxiety and promoting confidence.
Encourage self-reflection after assessments to help students identify strengths, weaknesses, and areas for improvement, fostering metacognition and independent learning.

Chapter 12: Testing the Learning Process

Mock Assessments: Discuss the importance of conducting practice tests and quizzes to prepare students for authentic assessments.

Reflective Practice: Encourage reflective practice to help students identify areas for improvement.

Chapter 12: Testing the Learning Process

Mastering the Assessment Landscape

Effective assessment is more than just a summative evaluation; it's a dynamic process that informs instruction and empowers students. This chapter explores strategies to enhance learning through strategic assessment practices.

Formative Assessment: Guiding Learning

Formative assessment is an ongoing, informal evaluation that provides feedback to both teachers and students to adjust instruction and learning strategies.

Critical components of formative assessment:

- **Observation:** Observing students' engagement, participation, and collaboration.
- **Questioning:** Asking probing questions to assess understanding.
- **Student self-assessment:** Encouraging students to reflect on their learning.
- **Peer assessment:** Having students provide feedback to each other.
- **Exit slips:** Gathering quick feedback at the end of a lesson.

Benefits of formative assessment:

- **Identifying student needs:** Teachers can pinpoint areas where students need support.
- **Differentiating instruction:** Teachers can tailor instruction to meet diverse learning needs.
- **Promoting student engagement:** Formative assessment makes learning more interactive and relevant.
- **Enhancing metacognition:** Students become more aware of their learning process.

Summative Assessment: Measuring Achievement

Each unit ends with a summative assessment or course to evaluate student learning outcomes. It provides comprehensive evidence of student achievement at a particular point in time.

Common types of summative assessment:

- **Standardized tests:** Large-scale assessments used for accountability purposes.
- **Unit tests:** Assessments covering specific content areas.
- **Projects and portfolios:** Demonstrations of student learning over time.
- **Performance assessments:** Students can apply knowledge and skills in real-world contexts.
- **Effective summative assessment:**
- **Alignment with learning objectives:** Ensure assessments measure what students have learned.
- **Reliability and validity:** Assessments should be consistent and accurate.
- **Clear scoring criteria:** Develop rubrics or checklists to guide evaluation.
- **Meaningful feedback**: Provide feedback that helps students improve.

A comprehensive assessment system effectively combines formative and summative assessments to support student learning and growth.

Assessment Tools and Technologies

Assessment tools and technologies have evolved significantly, offering educators various options to measure student learning effectively.

Digital Assessment Tools

- **Learning Management Systems (LMS):** Platforms like Canvas, Blackboard, and Google Classroom provide tools for creating quizzes, tests, and assignments. They offer automated grading, real-time feedback, and progress-tracking features.
- **Online Assessment Platforms:** Specialized platforms like Kahoot!, Quizlet, and Socrative offer interactive and engaging assessment options, including games, polls, and quizzes.

- **Adaptive Testing Software:** These tools adjust the difficulty of questions based on a student's performance, providing a more personalized assessment experience.
- **Performance-Based Assessment Tools**
- **Rubrics:** Detailed scoring guides that outline specific criteria for evaluating student work. They can be used for various assessments, including projects, presentations, and performances.
- **Checklists:** Simplified assessment tools that focus on specific skills or behaviors. They are often used for observational assessments or skill-based tasks.
- **Portfolios:** Collections of student work that demonstrate growth and achievement over time. Portfolios can be digital or physical.

Alternative Assessment Tools

- **Student Self-Assessment:** Tools that allow students to reflect on their learning and set goals. Journals, reflection prompts, and self-evaluation rubrics can be used.
- **Peer Assessment:** Students provide feedback to their classmates on specific criteria. This can foster collaboration and critical thinking.
- **Authentic Assessment:** Real-world tasks and projects that measure the ability of students' skill and knowledge in practical situations.

By incorporating various assessment tools and technologies, educators can create a comprehensive assessment system that provides valuable insights into student learning and informs instruction.

Selecting the Right Assessment Tools

Choosing the appropriate assessment tools is crucial for accurately measuring student learning and providing valuable feedback. Several factors influence the selection process:

- **Learning objectives:** Clearly defined learning outcomes determine the type of assessment needed. Performance-based assessments are suitable because they allow students to apply knowledge in a real-world context.
- **Student needs:** Consider students' diverse learning styles and abilities. A combination of assessment tools can accommodate different learners.

- **Assessment purpose:** Determine whether the assessment is formative, summative, or diagnostic. Each purpose requires different types of tools.
- **Practical considerations:** Factors such as time constraints, resources, and technology availability influence tool selection.

Matching Assessment Tools to Learning Objectives

Learning Objective	Assessment Tools
Knowledge recall	Multiple-choice tests, short answer questions
Comprehension	Essay questions, open-ended responses
Application	Projects, case studies, simulations
Analysis	Critical thinking questions, problem-solving tasks
Evaluation	Debates, research papers, portfolios
Creation	Product development, design projects, multimedia presentations

By carefully considering these factors, educators can select assessment tools that effectively measure student learning and provide meaningful feedback.

Using Assessment Data to Inform Instruction

Assessment data is a powerful tool for improving teaching and learning. By analyzing assessment results, educators can gain valuable insights into student strengths, weaknesses, and misconceptions.

Critical steps in using assessment data:

1. **Analyze the data:** Examine assessment results to identify patterns and trends. Look for areas where students are excelling and where they need additional support.
2. **Set goals:** Based on the data analysis, establish clear and measurable goals for student improvement.

3. **Differentiate instruction:** Tailor instruction to meet the specific needs of different learners. Use data to group students for targeted interventions or enrichment activities.

4. **Provide targeted feedback:** Offer specific and actionable feedback to students based on their assessment results.

5. **Adjust instruction:** Modify teaching strategies, materials, or activities to address areas where students are struggling.

6. **Monitor student progress:** Continuously assess student learning to track their progress and adjust as needed.

Example: Using Assessment Data to Improve Reading Comprehension

A teacher analyzes reading comprehension assessment data and discovers that many students need help identifying the main ideas. To address this, the teacher can:

- Provide explicit instruction on main idea identification strategies.
- Use graphic organizers to help students visualize the main ideas.
- Offer opportunities for students to practice identifying the main ideas in various texts.
- Provide targeted feedback on students' primary idea identification skills.

Teachers use assessment data to inform instruction, creating an environment that fosters engaging and creative learning opportunities for all students.

Chapter 13: Concluding with Learning

Celebrating achievements! Students share their newfound knowledge and skills.

Employ strategies like summarizing key points, reviewing practice problems, and providing additional resources to solidify learning and ensure long-term retention. Acknowledge and celebrate student achievements, big and small, to build confidence, motivation, and a positive learning environment where students feel valued and supported.

Chapter 13: Concluding with Learning

Reinforcement Strategies: Provide strategies for reviewing and reinforcing critical concepts at the end of each learning cycle.

Celebrating Success: Discuss the importance of recognizing and celebrating student achievements to foster a positive learning environment.

Chapter 13: Concluding with Learning: Building a Strong Foundation

The culmination of a learning unit presents a critical opportunity to solidify student understanding, reinforce key concepts, and prepare students for future learning. By strategically reinforcing acquired knowledge, educators can deepen students' comprehension, enhance retention, and foster a love of learning. This chapter explores practical techniques for consolidating learning, including the importance of revisiting and re-engaging students with the material in diverse ways. Through a combination of structured review, active learning strategies, and celebratory acknowledgments, teachers can create a powerful and lasting impact on student achievement. By building upon previously acquired knowledge and providing opportunities for students to apply their learning in new contexts, educators can establish a strong foundation for future academic success.

The following strategies can be adapted to various age groups and subjects:

Early Elementary (K-2)

- **Sensory Reinforcement:** Incorporate tactile, auditory, and visual elements to reinforce learning. For example, use flashcards with pictures and words, sing songs about math facts, or act out stories.
- **Game-Based Learning:** Create simple games that review concepts, such as matching games, board games, charades, and digital academic games.
- **Short, Frequent Reviews:** Conduct brief review sessions daily to reinforce critical concepts.

Upper Elementary (3-5)

- **Graphic Organizers:** Use graphic organizers like Venn diagrams, timelines, or concept maps to help students visualize relationships between ideas.

- **Peer Teaching:** Encourage students to explain concepts to each other in pairs or small groups.
- **Technology Integration:** Utilize educational apps or online games that reinforce learning.

Middle School (6-8)

- **Project-Based Learning:** Assign projects requiring students to apply learned concepts in the real world.
- **Study Groups:** Encourage students to form study groups to review material and quiz each other.
- **Concept Mapping:** Create complex concept maps to show the interconnectedness of ideas.

High School (9-12)

- **Advanced Organizers:** Provide students with outlines or summaries before new material to activate prior knowledge.
- **Debates and Discussions:** Engage students in debates or discussions to deepen understanding and critical thinking.
- **Real-world Applications:** Connect classroom learning to real-world scenarios to increase relevance.

Celebrating Success: Fostering a Positive Learning Environment

Celebrating student achievements is crucial for building confidence and motivation. Here are some strategies:

Early Elementary (K-2)

- **Individual Recognition:** Offer specific praise and encouragement to each student.
- **Tangible Rewards:** Use small, age-appropriate rewards like stickers, pencils, or extra playtime.
- **Class Celebrations:** Celebrate collective achievements with simple parties or activities.

Upper Elementary (3-5)

- **Peer Recognition:** Implement a system where students can nominate classmates for achievements.
- **Goal Setting and Achievement:** Help students set and track goals, celebrating milestones.
- **Themed Celebrations:** Organize themed celebrations based on academic achievements, such as a "Math Magician" day or a "Reading Rainbow" week.

Middle School (6-8)

- **Student-Led Celebrations:** Empower students to plan and organize celebrations for their classmates.
- **Academic Awards:** Create awards for outstanding achievement in different subjects or areas.
- **Growth Mindset Emphasis:** Celebrate improvement and effort in addition to accomplishments.

High School (9-12)

- **Public Recognition:** Showcase student work or achievements on a school website or bulletin board.
- **College and Career Readiness Celebrations:** Highlight students' accomplishments related to college applications or career goals.
- **Mentorship Programs:** Pair successful students with younger students to foster a sense of community and shared success.

By implementing these strategies, educators can create a classroom environment where students feel valued, motivated, and empowered to reach their full potential.

Conclusion

Conclusion:
Chapter 14: The Future of Education

Empowered and ready! Intentional teaching shapes the next generation of learners.

Chapter 14: The Future of Education

The Impact of Teaching Differently: Reflect on how the Teach Differently Intentionally framework can transform education.

Next Steps for Educators: Provide practical advice for educators on implementing this methodology in their classrooms.

Final Thoughts: Offer encouragement and motivation for educators embarking on this transformative journey.

Chapter 14:
The Future of Education

The Impact of Teaching Differently Intentionally

Student-centered learning is a phrase often echoed in educational circles. Yet, the true essence of placing students at the heart of the learning process requires a deliberate, intentional shift in pedagogy. The Teach Differently Intentionally framework is more than just a concept; it's a roadmap to transform classrooms into dynamic, engaging spaces where students are active participants, not passive recipients of information. It necessitates a profound departure from traditional teaching methods, demanding educators rethink their roles, redefine student experiences, and cultivate a culture of inquiry and exploration. More than merely discussing student-centered learning is required; we can truly unlock students' full potential through intentional action and a deep commitment to this framework.

Next Steps for Educators

Embarking on the Teaching Differently Intentionally journey requires courage, perseverance, and a commitment to continuous learning. Start by identifying specific areas for growth and development. Consider joining professional learning communities or attending conferences to connect with like-minded educators. Experiment with new teaching strategies, but remember to reflect on their effectiveness. Celebrate small victories along the way and seek feedback from students and colleagues. Trust your instincts and adapt the framework to fit your unique classroom context.

Final Thoughts

Teaching is a noble profession that demands constant growth and adaptation. The Teaching Differently Intentionally framework provides a roadmap for educators to create learning environments that intentionally allow students to experience their learning journey. Remember, every small step towards intentional teaching brings you closer to creating a classroom where students are inspired, engaged, and empowered. Embrace the challenges, celebrate the successes, and never lose sight of your passion for teaching. The future of education is in your hands.

By adopting the Teaching Differently Intentionally framework, educators can become catalysts for change and inspire a new generation of critical thinkers, problem-solvers, and lifelong learners.

Notes:

Appendices

Appendix

"I touch the future. I teach."
-Christa McAuliffe

Intentional teaching empowers educators to create a dynamic learning environment where every student thrives, unlocking the door to a future where education is truly transformative and every child flourishes.

Imagine a classroom where every student thrives, where learning is not just a task but an exciting journey of discovery. This is the power of intentional teaching, a transformative approach that empowers educators to create a dynamic learning environment where every student feels seen, heard, and supported.
In this vibrant space, teachers are not just instructors but facilitators of knowledge, guiding students toward their full potential."
Intentional teaching unlocks a future where every student excels and embraces challenges."
This is not just an ideal but a reality within reach, a future where education is truly transformative and every child flourishes.

I believe in you; go forth and Teach Differently and Intentionally.

Alisa L. Grace

Appendix A:
Sample Survey for Learning Styles

A sample survey that educators can use to assess their students' learning preferences.

Appendix A:
Sample Survey for Learning Styles

Note: This survey is designed to provide insights into students' learning preferences. It is essential to remember that individuals are complex learners and may exhibit multiple learning styles.

Student Learning Style Survey

Please answer the following questions carefully to help us understand how you learn best.

Instructions

Circle the number that best represents your agreement with each statement.

1. Strongly Disagree
2. Disagree
3. Neutral
4. Agree
5. Strongly Agree

Visual Learner

- I learn best by seeing things, such as pictures, diagrams, or charts. (1, 2, 3, 4, 5)
- I remember information better when it is presented visually. (1, 2, 3, 4, 5)
- I enjoy using maps, graphs, and timelines. (1, 2, 3, 4, 5)

Auditory Learner

- I learn best by hearing information, such as lectures or discussions. (1, 2, 3, 4, 5)
- I remember information better when it is spoken aloud. (1, 2, 3, 4, 5)
- I enjoy listening to music, podcasts, or audiobooks. (1, 2, 3, 4, 5)

Kinesthetic Learner

- I learn best by doing things and moving around. (1, 2, 3, 4, 5)
- I remember information better when I am physically active. (1, 2, 3, 4, 5)
- I enjoy hands-on activities and experiments. (1, 2, 3, 4, 5)

Read/Write Learner

- I learn best by reading and writing information. (1, 2, 3, 4, 5)
- I remember information better when I take notes or write it down. (1, 2, 3, 4, 5)
- I enjoy reading books, articles, and essays. (1, 2, 3, 4, 5)

Social Learner

- I learn best by working with others and sharing ideas. (1, 2, 3, 4, 5)
- I remember information better when I discuss it with others. (1, 2, 3, 4, 5)
- I enjoy group projects and activities. (1, 2, 3, 4, 5)

Solitary Learner

- I learn best by working independently and quietly. (1, 2, 3, 4, 5)
- I remember information better when I study alone. (1, 2, 3, 4, 5)
- I enjoy working on individual projects. (1, 2, 3, 4, 5)

Technology Preferences

- I prefer learning with technology tools like computers, tablets, or smartphones. (1, 2, 3, 4, 5)
- I find online videos and tutorials helpful. (1, 2, 3, 4, 5)
- I enjoy using educational apps and software. (1, 2, 3, 4, 5)

Learning Environment Preferences

- I prefer a quiet and calm learning environment. (1, 2, 3, 4, 5)
- I prefer a learning environment with background noise. (1, 2, 3, 4, 5)
- I learn best in a collaborative and social learning environment. (1, 2, 3, 4, 5)
- I prefer a flexible and adaptable learning environment. (1, 2, 3, 4, 5)

Additional Questions:

- What study methods do you find most effective?
- Do you prefer to work in groups or individually?
- How do you typically organize your notes and materials?
- What types of activities help you stay focused and engaged?
- How do you use technology to support your learning?
- What kind of learning environment do you find most conducive to your learning?

Note: This survey can be adapted to suit specific age groups and educational levels. Consider adding questions about specific technology tools or learning platforms.

Remember: This survey provides insights into learning preferences, but observing students in different contexts is essential to understanding their learning styles comprehensively.

Appendix B:
Sample Rubrics

Include examples of rubrics that can be used to evaluate student projects based on the framework's principles.

Appendix B: Sample Rubrics

Rubrics are tools that provide clear criteria for evaluating student work. They can be used to assess various projects and assignments and tailored to specific learning objectives. The following are examples of rubrics that align with the Teach Differently Intentionally framework.

Rubric 1: Student-Centered Project

This rubric evaluates a project that emphasizes student agency and creativity.

Criteria	Exemplary	Proficient	Developing	Beginning
Student Agency	Demonstrates exceptional project ownership, makes independent decisions, and seeks feedback effectively.	Shows strong evidence of ownership, makes informed decisions, and seeks feedback when needed.	Shows some evidence of ownership, makes decisions with guidance, and seeks limited feedback.	Lacks evidence of ownership, relies heavily on teacher direction, and seeks minimal feedback.
Creativity and Innovation	Presents a highly original and creative solution to the problem, demonstrating exceptional problem-solving skills.	Presents a creative solution to the problem, demonstrating strong problem-solving skills.	Presents a creative solution to the problem, demonstrating basic problem-solving skills.	Lacks creativity and originality and needs to demonstrate more problem-solving skills.
Depth of Knowledge	Demonstrates a deep understanding of the subject, incorporating complex ideas and connections.	Demonstrates a solid understanding of the subject matter, incorporating key concepts.	Demonstrates a basic understanding of the subject matter, with some superficial knowledge.	Demonstrates limited understanding of the subject matter, with factual errors.
Collaboration and Communication	Effectively collaborates with peers, communicates clearly and persuasively, and demonstrates leadership.	Collaborates effectively with peers, communicates clearly, and contributes to group success.	Participates in group work, communicates adequately, and requires some guidance.	Struggles to collaborate, communicates ineffectively, and relies heavily on others.

Rubric 2: Inquiry-Based Learning Project

This rubric evaluates a project that emphasizes critical thinking and problem-solving.

Criteria	Exemplary	Proficient	Developing	Beginning
Inquiry Skills	Demonstrates exceptional ability to formulate research questions, gather evidence, and analyze data.	Demonstrates strong ability to formulate research questions, gather relevant evidence, and analyze data.	Demonstrates basic ability to formulate research questions and gather some evidence.	Struggles to formulate research questions and gather relevant evidence.
Critical Thinking	Demonstrates exceptional critical thinking skills, evaluating evidence and drawing insightful conclusions.	Demonstrates strong critical thinking skills, analyzing evidence, and drawing sound conclusions.	Demonstrates basic critical thinking skills, identifying some patterns in the data.	Struggles to think critically and draw meaningful conclusions.
Communication	Effectively communicates findings through clear and persuasive presentations or written reports.	Communicates findings clearly and effectively through presentations or written reports.	Communicates findings with some clarity but needs more persuasiveness.	Struggles to communicate findings effectively, with significant errors.
Reflection	Demonstrates deep reflection on the learning process, identifying strengths, weaknesses, and areas for growth.	Demonstrates thoughtful reflection on the learning process, identifying key learnings.	Demonstrates some reflection on the learning process but needs more depth.	Shows little evidence of reflection on the learning process.

These rubrics can be adapted to fit specific projects and grade levels. Involving students in the rubric development is essential to fostering ownership and understanding of the assessment criteria.

Rubric 1: Mathematics Project

This rubric evaluates a mathematics project emphasizing problem-solving, critical thinking, and communication.

Criteria	Exemplary	Proficient	Developing	Beginning
Mathematical Understanding	Demonstrates a deep understanding of mathematical concepts and applies them accurately to solve complex problems.	Demonstrates a solid understanding of mathematical concepts and applies them to solve problems with some accuracy.	Demonstrates a basic understanding of mathematical concepts but needs help with application.	Demonstrates limited understanding of mathematical concepts and makes frequent errors.
Problem-Solving	Demonstrates exceptional problem-solving skills, using multiple strategies and persevering through challenges.	Demonstrates strong problem-solving skills, using a variety of strategies to find solutions.	Demonstrates basic problem-solving skills but relies heavily on procedural knowledge.	Struggles with problem-solving and relies on teacher guidance.
Communication	Clearly and effectively communicates mathematical ideas and reasoning through written and oral presentations.	Communicates mathematical ideas clearly, with some minor errors in presentation.	Communicates mathematical ideas with difficulty and needs more clarity.	Struggles to communicate mathematical ideas, with significant errors.
Creativity and Innovation	Demonstrates exceptional creativity and originality in approaching the problem and exploring multiple solutions.	Demonstrates creativity and originality in approaching the problem by exploring different methods.	Shows some creativity but relies on familiar approaches.	Lacks creativity and originality, following a prescribed method.

Rubric 2: Science Experiment

This rubric evaluates a science experiment emphasizing inquiry, data analysis, and communication.

Criteria	Exemplary	Proficient	Developing	Beginning
Scientific Inquiry	Demonstrates exceptional ability to formulate a clear research question, develop a controlled experiment, and collect accurate data.	Demonstrates strong ability to formulate a research question, design an experiment, and collect relevant data.	Demonstrates basic ability to formulate a research question and experiment with some errors.	Struggles to formulate a research question and conduct a valid experiment.
Data Analysis	Demonstrates exceptional ability to analyze data, identify patterns, and draw accurate conclusions.	Demonstrates strong ability to analyze data, identify trends, and draw reasonable conclusions.	Demonstrates basic ability to analyze data but needs help to draw meaningful conclusions.	Struggles to analyze data and draw conclusions.
Communication	Effectively communicates experimental procedures, data, and findings through clear, organized reports or presentations.	Communicates experimental procedures, data, and findings clearly, with minor errors.	Communicates experimental procedures and data with difficulty and needs more clarity.	Struggles to communicate experimental procedures and findings, with significant errors.
Critical Thinking	Demonstrates exceptional critical thinking skills, evaluating evidence and considering alternative explanations.	Demonstrates strong critical thinking skills, analyzing data to support conclusions.	Demonstrates basic critical thinking skills but needs to improve to evaluate evidence critically.	Lacks critical thinking skills and relies on superficial observations.

Rubric 3: Social Studies Project

This rubric evaluates a social studies project emphasizing research, critical thinking, and communication.

Criteria	Exemplary	Proficient	Developing	Beginning
Historical Understanding	Demonstrates a deep understanding of historical context, using multiple sources to support claims.	Demonstrates a solid understanding of historical context, using relevant sources.	Demonstrates a basic understanding of historical context but relies on limited sources.	Demonstrates limited understanding of historical context, with factual errors.
Research Skills	Demonstrates exceptional research skills, gathering information from a variety of credible sources.	Demonstrates strong research skills, gathering relevant information from multiple sources.	Demonstrates basic research skills but relies on limited sources.	Struggles with research with limited information gathered.
Critical Thinking	Demonstrates exceptional critical thinking skills, analyzing information, and forming well-supported arguments.	Demonstrates strong critical thinking skills, evaluating evidence and drawing informed conclusions.	Demonstrates basic critical thinking skills but needs help to analyze information effectively.	Lacks critical thinking skills and relies on superficial information.
Communication	Effectively communicates findings through clear and engaging presentations or written reports.	Communicates findings clearly and effectively, with some minor errors.	Communicates findings with some clarity but needs more organization.	Struggles to communicate findings, with significant errors.

Rubric 4: Language Arts Project

This rubric evaluates a language arts project emphasizing reading comprehension, writing, and communication.

Criteria	Exemplary	Proficient	Developing	Beginning
Reading Comprehension	Demonstrates exceptional comprehension of complex texts, making insightful connections and inferences.	Demonstrates strong comprehension of texts, making relevant connections and inferences.	Demonstrates basic comprehension of texts but needs help to make connections.	Struggles to comprehend texts with limited understanding.
Writing	Produces exceptional writing that is clear, coherent, and engaging, with strong use of language.	Produces strong writing that is clear and organized, with effective use of language.	Produces writing that is generally clear but needs more organization and clarity.	Produces writing that is difficult to understand, with frequent errors.
Communication	Effectively communicates ideas and information through oral presentations or written reports.	Communicates ideas clearly and effectively, with some minor errors.	Communicates ideas with some clarity but needs more organization.	Struggles to communicate ideas, with significant errors.
Creativity	Demonstrates exceptional creativity and originality in expressing ideas, using vivid language and imagery.	Demonstrates creativity and originality in expressing ideas using descriptive language.	Shows some creativity but relies on familiar writing styles.	Lacks creativity and originality, with limited use of language.

These rubrics can be adapted to fit specific grade levels, learning objectives, and project requirements. Providing students with clear and specific rubric criteria and feedback is essential.

Notes:

Appendix C:
Resources for Interactive Activities

Educators can use resources to create interactive and engaging learning experiences, including books, websites, and tools.

Appendix C: Resources for Interactive Activities

Online Platforms and Tools

- **Learning Management Systems (LMS):** Canvas, Blackboard, Google Classroom
- **Interactive Whiteboards:** Promethean ActivBoard, SMART Board
- **Video Conferencing:** Zoom, Google Meet, Microsoft Teams
- **Online Assessment Tools:** Kahoot!, Quizlet, Socrative
- **Educational Games and Simulations:** PhET Interactive Simulations, BrainPOP, National Geographic Kids
- **Digital Storytelling Tools:** Storybird, WeVideo, Adobe Spark
- **Graphic Organizers:** Coggle, Miro, Lucidchart
- **Collaborative Tools:** Google Docs, Padlet, Trello

Websites and Online Resources

- **Educational Websites:** National Geographic, Scholastic, NASA
- **Open Educational Resources (OER):** Khan Academy, OpenStax, MERLOT
- **Online Libraries:** Digital Public Library of America, Internet Archive
- **Educational Databases:** EBSCO, JSTOR, ScienceDirect

Books and Print Materials

- **Children's Literature:** Picture books, chapter books, graphic novels
- **Reference Books:** Encyclopedias, atlases, dictionaries
- **Non-fiction Books:** Science, history, biography, and other informational texts
- **Manipulatives:** Math manipulatives, science kits, building blocks
- **Art Supplies:** Paints, crayons, markers, clay, construction paper

Technology Hardware

- **Computers:** Desktops, laptops, tablets
- **Projectors:** Interactive whiteboards, document cameras
- **Audio Equipment:** Microphones, speakers
- **Video Equipment:** Cameras, video recorders
- **Robotics and Coding Kits:** Lego Mindstorms, Arduino, Raspberry Pi

Community Resources

- **Museums and Science Centers:** Hands-on exhibits, educational programs
- **Zoos and Aquariums:** Animal encounters, educational programs
- **Historical Sites:** Guided tours, reenactments
- **Local Businesses and Organizations:** Guest speakers, field trips, internships

Note: This list can be adapted to specific grade levels and subject areas. Careful evaluation of learning resources created to align with learning objectives is essential.

Notes:

Appendix D:
Reflection and Progress Monitoring Tools

Provide templates and tools for educators to use in progress monitoring and student reflection.

Appendix D:
Reflection and Progress Monitoring Tools

Understanding Reflection and Progress Monitoring

Reflection and progress monitoring are essential components of effective teaching and learning. They provide valuable insights into student growth, inform instructional planning, and foster a culture of continuous improvement. By involving students in the reflection and monitoring process, educators can empower them to take ownership of their learning and develop metacognitive skills.

Student Reflection Tools

Student Self-Assessment

Learning Journal: A dedicated notebook for students to record their thoughts, questions, and reflections on their learning process.

Example prompt: "What did I learn today? What questions do I still have?"

Goal Setting Worksheet: A structured tool for students to identify learning goals, track progress, and celebrate achievements.

Example:

- Learning Goal:
- Steps to achieve goal:
- Evidence of progress:
- Challenges faced:
- Celebrations:

Traffic Light System: A simple visual tool for students to self-assess their understanding of a topic.

Green: I understand the concept fully.
Yellow: I understand most of the concepts but need more practice.
Red: I need help understanding the concept.

Student-Created Reflection Questions

To encourage deeper reflection, students can develop their questions to consider after completing a lesson or unit.

Example prompts:

What was the most challenging aspect of this lesson/unit?
How did I overcome obstacles in my learning?
What new connections did I make between this topic and other subjects?
How can I apply what I learned to a real-world situation?

Peer Assessment

Peer Feedback Form: A structured tool for students to provide feedback to classmates on specific criteria.

Example criteria: Clarity, creativity, collaboration, content knowledge.

Teacher Progress Monitoring Tools

Anecdotal Records

Observation Notes: Brief observations of student behavior, engagement, and learning progress.

Example: "John actively participated in today's group discussion, sharing insightful ideas."

Checklist

Skill Checklist: A list of specific skills or behaviors to observe and document.

Example: For reading, checklist items might include fluency, comprehension, and vocabulary.

Rubrics

Project Rubric: Detailed criteria for evaluating student projects, as outlined in Appendix B.

Performance Rubric: Criteria for assessing student performance on specific tasks or skills.

Data Tracking Sheet

Progress Monitoring Chart: A chart to track student performance on specific skills or assessments.

Example: A graph to track reading fluency scores.

Collaborative Reflection Tools

Group Reflection: A structured discussion or activity for students and teachers to collectively reflect on learning experiences.

Portfolio Assessment: Student work showcasing growth and learning over time.

Student-Teacher Conferences: Regular meetings to discuss student progress, goals, and challenges.

By utilizing these tools, educators can gain valuable insights into student learning, make data-driven instructional decisions, and create a culture of reflection and growth. Involving students in the reflection process empowers them to take ownership of their knowledge and develop metacognitive skills.

Goal Setting Worksheet

My Learning Journey

Name: **Date:**

Learning Goal: *Clearly and specifically state what you want to achieve.*

Steps to Achieve Goal: *Break down the goal into smaller, manageable steps. 1. 2. 3. 4. 5.*

Evidence of Progress: *How will you know if you are progressing towards your goal?*

      Track your efforts and achievements here.*

Challenges Faced: *Identify any obstacles or difficulties you encounter. Describe how you overcame or plan to overcome these challenges.*

Celebrations: *Recognize and reward your accomplishments. Celebrate your successes, no matter how small.*

Notes:

Student-Created Reflection Questions Form

Reflect on your learning:

- What was the most challenging aspect of this lesson/unit?
- How did I overcome obstacles in my learning?
- What new connections did I make between this topic and other subjects?
- How can I apply what I learned to a real-world situation?
- What surprised me about this topic?
- What questions do I still have about this content?
- How did my thinking change as I learned more about this topic?
- What would I do differently if I could do this project again?
- How did working with others contribute to my learning?
- What strategies did I use to help me understand the material?

Remember: These are just starting points. Feel free to create your questions that reflect your personal learning experience.

Notes:

Peer Feedback Form

Student Name:

Project/Assignment:

Peer Reviewer Name:

Please provide constructive feedback to help your classmate improve their work.

Criteria

Clarity: How well is the information presented? Is it easy to understand?

Specific feedback:

Creativity: How original and imaginative is the work?

Specific feedback:

Collaboration: How well did the student work with others?

Specific feedback:

Content Knowledge: How well does the work demonstrate understanding of the subject matter?

Specific feedback:

Overall Impression

What do you think are the strengths of this project?

What suggestions do you have for improvement?

Remember: Effective feedback is specific and helpful. Focus on sharing actionable feedback to help your classmate grow as a learner.

This book serves as a comprehensive guide for educators seeking to transform their teaching practices by adopting the Teaching Differently Intentionally framework. It offers practical strategies, real-world examples, and resources to support their journey.

Meet the Author: Alisa Ladawn Grace

Alisa Ladawn Grace is a seasoned educator and transformational life coach with a profound commitment to empowering children. She has a Specialist degree in Curriculum and Instruction and brings over two decades of experience in Exceptional Student Education, Reading Coaching, Instructional Coaching, and school administration. Her tenure as Chief Operating Officer of a non-profit organization further honed her leadership and strategic planning skills.

Alisa's dedication to fostering civic engagement in young minds is evident in her children's books: "Civic Heroes: Discovering Elections with the Supervisor of Elections," "My Civic Adventure: Learning About Voting and Community!", and "Election Essentials with the Supervisor of Elections: A Guide to Civics for Young Citizens." These engaging works introduce complex political concepts in an age-appropriate manner.

Beyond civic education, Alisa's book, "Unlocking Your Great Potential Within You: A Comprehensive Curriculum Guide to Nurturing Children's Meditation, Executive Functioning, and Good Habits," offers practical strategies for parents and educators to cultivate well-rounded individuals. This curriculum guide emphasizes the power of meditation, critical thinking, and character development in shaping young minds.

Alisa's passion for education and child development is the driving force behind her work. She is dedicated to positively impacting young people's lives and inspiring them to thrive as they reach their full potential as responsible citizens and individuals.

Ready to make learning an adventure? This guide is your passport to a more engaging, practical, personalized learning experience. Whether you're a teacher looking to shake things up in your classroom or a parent guiding your child's learning at home, this guide is packed with tools and strategies that will make every student and child shine. We'll show you how to create lessons that spark curiosity, ignite passion, and help each student and child discover their unique strengths. Get ready to transform education and unlock your student's and child's full potential.

Have you ever wondered how to truly connect with every student and child? Or how to make lessons so exciting that kids can't wait to learn? Ready to help your student and child discover their unique path to success? This guide is here to help you do just that and so much more.

www.ingramcontent.com/pod-product-compliance
Lightning Source LLC
Chambersburg PA
CBHW080806300426
44114CB00020B/2852